Tales of the Internet

Jessica Keyes

Jessica Keyes

Revised edition 2019. Original published as The Human Web in 2001.

TABLE OF CONTENTS

@SEX

One of my favorite movies is Woody Allen's *Sleeper.* In this 1973 sleeper of a comedy, a man who was cryogenically frozen is reawakened to a future that includes Orgasmatron booths to replace sex. Far-fetched? Not according to Joel C. Snell, a Fellow at the Arlington Institute. Snell thinks that virtual sex is coming soon to a computer near you,

In virtual sex ... the voyeuristic pleasure of watching people engage in coital capers .. .is replaced by providing the realism of the user participating in the action. The user puts on a helmet of or gets into a large box ... Virtual sex will not necessarily be confined to establishment sex parlors .... The bulge you see in a traveler's briefcase may not be a weighty report but a two-way virtual sex unit...

Of course, the future's got nothing on the present where sex is concerned. It's all around us. Sex-charged commercials, movies and television shows. Go into any magazine store and you'll see dozens of male-oriented magazines. Even in staid merry old England, where these magazines where long relegated to the back room, glossies with ladies in full bloom are in full view.

The arrival of girl-power feminism in the 1980s, with Madonna as Queen of the boy-toys, made it okay to use your sexuality to sell yourself. It seems that taking your clothes off is no longer degrading but "empowering" to women and fully endorsed by famous pro-porn feminists as Erica Jong and Camille Paglia.

There's even a popular nightclub in New York City where hip partygoers are lining up to strip naked and perform sexual acts. All ages, shapes, sexes, income and educational levels seem to love to get involved. A 35-year old college philosophy lecturer handed a pair of scissors to a crowd member to cut loose her fishnet pantyhose. She later cut a hole in the crotch area.

People have been repressed in New York - the clubs have been cracked down upon - and now people are busting loose with what's underneath.

It's interesting to note that before stripping on stage the revelers were required to sign release forms that allowed event organizers to use the film and photographs on the Internet. Said Matthew Heindl, a marketing manager for an Internet reality-show,

Everyone likes their 15 minutes of fame - in the Internet they'll have 15 seconds. I hope there are no future Senate candidates out there.

Unfortunately, our government, including the White House, is no longer above this sort of behavior.

Ply was put up for adoption at age 12 by her Cambodian mother who could simply no longer afford to provide for her children. Told that she was going to work as a maid, Ply was instead driven to a Phnom Penh hotel where she was auctioned off into sex slavery. For sexual predators Cambodia is paradise. Decades of war have left the country one of the poorest, worst educated and most corrupt in the world. With an average wage of under $300 a year, a family unit that no longer exists and a life expectancy under 60, life is cheap.

The sexual revolution underbelly is not limited to the third world. Vancouver is one of the most beautiful of cities in North America. Located between the Coast mountains and the Pacific Ocean, the skyscrapers of this major Canadian city seem to sparkle. Voted one of the most desirable cities in the world, it is also home to a deep dark secret. For just past trendy Gastown you will find a Vancouver where sex, drugs and booze are the business of the day - and night.

For it is night when the women, some as young as 14, start trolling the street, all but oblivious to the danger all around them. Since 1978 at least dozens of them have disappeared, most of them since 1997. No trace of any of them has ever been found.

Sarah deVries is one of these girls. Missing since 1998, she left a diary that shows how rough and dangerous life in the area called Low Track is.

I got in, pulled the door shut and agreed on 40 .... His name I don 't remember or maybe I just don 't want to. Anyway I told him my name Sarah, and it all started at that moment .... Sarah this and Sarah that, it started to scare the hell out of me, it was like he was trying to psyche himself up to do something.

Vancouver has acquired a global reputation as a "hotspot" for pedophiles and other sex criminals. Indeed, it is not uncommon for johns to be stopped and found to have what are called "kill kits" - knife, rope and plastic bags.

While predatory sex and violent endings have always been an undercurrent to our civilized world - think Jack the Ripper and the Rape of the Sabine women - one can rightfully question the role the Internet plays in the escalation of these crimes.

All sex, all the time. In the old days a man needing some gratification had to endure the embarrassment of donning his trench coat and making a very visible foray to his local adult video store. Today he can just slink to his den and by the green glow of his laptop or mobile device draw on the seemingly limitless collection of the Internet.

NetDoctor.co.uk surveyed British 850 adults and found that 25 percent of the men and 15% of the women claimed to have had Internet sex. And that's probably on the low side. The Illinois Institute for Addiction Recovery puts the number of addicted Internet users at 5%-10% of those online. These folks engage in their little peccadilloes by exchanging pornographic images through various Internet portals, including Facebook and the Dark Web.

All genders, all nationalities and all income levels seem to be hooked on porn, although the vast majority of them are men. A beloved doctor in Massachusetts was convicted of murder in 2001. Dr. Dirk Greineder led a double life. Life saver in the morning and life snuffer in the night. The trial uncovered the gruesome details of the prostitutes the good doctor slept with at roadside motels, the Internet sex sites he visited, and the naked photo of himself that he sent to prospective sex partners.

Shana Marie Lawson, an Ohio woman, was sentenced to five years in federal prison in 2001 for luring a 15-year old girl into a sexual affair. Lawson developed the relationship with the teen through Internet messages.

Peter Gulotta is a special agent with the Baltimore division of the FBI. Assigned to the *Innocent Images Project* his job is to track down online perverts under whatever rock they're hiding. Problem is that most of these fellows - and they are mostly fellows - don't look like perverts. Gulotta says that, "these are people who live next to you and me .... Their profile is white male, 25-45 years old, has a better than average income, better than average intelligence, and has never been charged with crimes against children or even suspected of any crimes against children .... ". Over the years the FBI has arrested a pediatrician, a Broadway producer, a Diplomat, law enforcement officers, and even an elementary school principal. This FBI unit started back in the mid nineties and since then its case load has grown exponentially.

This project started in our division because of a case about a young boy by the name of George Burdinski. He was a 10 year old boy that lived with his parents in Brentwood, Maryland. He was abducted from his neighborhood in 1993 and was never found. The case is still unsolved. During the course of the investigation, the FBI, in conjunction with the local police department, came across a couple of suspects who, although they were not charged in this case, were routinely using the Internet to try to lure young boys in the Mid-Atlantic region into having sex and they were also transmitting images of child porn   We came up with an idea of running an undercover operation that would deal with people like that - individuals who get online and contact whom they think are children and then travel interstate with the intention of having sex with them ..... And the second group of people are the group that actually transmit the images of child pornography, bearing in mind that even the mere possession of it is an offense.

We have agents that go online into what we call predicated chat rooms posing as children. These are chat rooms where we believe there are people looking to have sex with kids or are looking to trade images of child porn ..... In short order of logging on these guys will see what they think is a kid and they'll engage us in a private area ..... Soon they're sending us pornography or at least they're talking about what they'd like to do ... When they express an interest in having sex .... and arrive at a prearranged destination they are charged with traveling interstate with the intention of having sex with a minor ....

Agent Gulotta doesn't know whether these rising statistics mean that's it's getting worse or just that's coming out from where's its been hiding all these years. What I know is that these are the real "X-Files".

If sex can be likened to a locust then the Internet is surely plagued. You can't escape it, no matter how you try. One of my clients even called me up the other day to tell me that a slight variation of my company's name typed into a browser brings up an interesting web site where a man can buy a contraption to pump up his pride and joy.

Back in the early 2000's, prior to the rise of social media, there were 281,000 discussion threads in the alt.sex newsgroup. I found only 36,000 for education and 47,000 for love. This has only grown since the advent of Facebook and the Dark Web,

I get about 10 e-mails a day with come hither subjects like "20 photos of brunette spreading long legs", but that's only the tip of the iceberg. I surveyed some of these sites when doing research for this chapter. These sites contain twosomes and threesomes, Asian beauties, bestiality, and lots and lots of pictures of women in poses that only their gynecologists should ever hope to see. Virtual Peeping Toms have a 24x7 show. Even college girls are in the act with some Sorority houses outfitted with up to 70 webcams in all the most unlikely places.

Since women make Internet porn go around, one most pose a question about why so many girls are doing so many bad things online (and off). It can't just be a money thing. Dr. Lorraine Nencel teaches courses and does research in anthropology. One of the things she studies is prostitutes. Here's what she has to say about this complex topic,

It depends if you want to look at prostitution, live porno, virtual porno only in terms of degradation, abuse, then it is definitely difficult to grasp it. And that is a part of the whole debate in States: are these things harmful to women, producing repression, etc or are these a women's choice, right to choose and in some sense liberating?

There are many examples where you see that they are pretty

much hometown girls. Sometimes there are sort of biographies on television and you hear them talking about their work as porno stars as a job even a career. Do you get the program Ruby Wax in the states? Well she is an American living in England and does all these interviews. She followed a group of porno stars around for a whole day and she gave a pretty good picture of how they felt about it, at the same time she showed her difficulty in dealing with it.

I read an article on female strippers in a strip joint written by a sociologist. She showed how the power relation was two ways and the constraints too. Both the women and men gain a sort of power in the interaction but at the same time felt the negative side. So it isn't so clear cut.

The funny thing about the Internet and porn is that the porn industry seems to front-wheel drive the Internet. In other words video, web casting, subscription payment models were all first used on porn sites only later to be adopted by the more traditional sites. Porn has even make its way to a handheld device near you. A start-up named Erotigo is working hard to become the premier provider of mobile adult entertainment. Soon an on-the-go business executive - male or female - can oh-so easily login and jack-off.

So it's no wonder that you can get whatever you want and whenever you want it on the Internet - wired or wireless. There are even web sites where clients can view a woman, who is being videotaped, and issue instructions. Prospective clients log into a chat room and may then "move" to a private room where the instructions may be issued. The client can also video himself, with the images transmitted live by video-streaming technology.

While this might be fine among consenting adults, as the Vancouver and Cambodia stories above attest to, not everyone involved in this business consents to their exploitation.

A California girl of eight, attending a sleepover party at a friend's home, was raped to order by her friend's father for the entertainment of a dozen pedophiles logged onto the Internet in four different countries. Members of this sexual cabal sent typed messages which appeared on Ronald Riva's computer screen asking him to perform particular sexual acts on the girl.

Nine-year old Mary did what children do best. She annoyed her next door neighbor by writing with chalk on his driveway. But her neighbor was perverted and he was hooked to the Internet. As Mary's mother tells it,

The phone awakened me from a sound sleep, and I was confused about why a grown man would want to talk to my 9-year old daughter at three in the morning .... Over the next few weeks, the calls continued. Day and night, men wanted to talk to our little girl Was there something concerning Mary on the Internet. When Mike used our
phone number as the "key" for searching newsgroups he found 14 matches .... Most of the messages implied that our daughter was having sex with her father and said outright that she wanted to have sex with other men.

In 1997, at the time this happened, there were no laws making it illegal to post a minor's name and phone number on Internet sex boards. Because of the persistence and diligence of Mary's mother there now is.

This, sad to say, is quite a common occurrence. In Bangkok, after a young graduate student disappeared, her mother began receiving hundreds of phone calls from men wanting to have sex with the missing girl. The men claimed they got the phone number from a sex trade websites.

There was a story just yesterday about a guy who went to meet a girl he had an internet relationship with and he ended up murdered. The "girl" was a guy who just lured him there to kill him.

Internet urban legend or real thing? Who knows, but

what we do know is that looking for love on the Internet might be a case of looking for love in all the wrong places. Those doing the dirty deed and getting caught are now coming up with a novel defense. Patrick Naughton was a vice president of Walt Disney's go.com. He had been chatting with, what he thought to be, a 13-year old girl in the "Dad&DaughterSex" Internet chat room. But then they decided to meet. Naughton flew from his home in Seattle salivating at the thought of his rendezvous at the Santa Monica pier. The 13-year old turned out to be a cop working undercover and Naughton was arrested and charged with traveling across state lines to have sex with a minor and enticing a minor to have sex by using the Internet.

Next comes the creative defense. His clever attorneys argued that their client lacked the requisite mental state to commit the crimes. Instead, they asserted that Mr. Naughton was participating in an Internet sex fantasy and had no real intent to have sex with a minor. They said that he traveled all that distance just to see who his counterpart was in the role-playing world of Internet sex fantasies. After all, these lawyers contend, the Internet is a world in which a gorgeous 19-year old girl in a chat room is almost always a 14-year old pimply boy goofing on the other participants.

Interestingly, the jury hung on the decision. It was divided along gender lines. The men asserted that Mr. Naughton was playing out an innocent fantasy, while the women believed that the defendant had gone to the pier with the intent of having sex with a child.

I wonder? Did the prosecution ask how many potential jurors engaged in Internet sex during the voir dire?

While the American Psychiatric Association contends that there is no such thing as a sex junkie, more and more people are being diagnosed with what is usually referred to as a sex addiction.

Whether sexual addition (think Jeffrey Epstein) is caused by constant sexual stimulation which conditions the brain to desire even more sexual stimulation or is the result of some deep-seated childhood trauma or psychological condition such as depression, it is most certainly habit-forming. And has some pretty severe consequences as Dr. Harvey Asher describes,

Cybersex addicts' brains are probably getting all kinds of endorphin reactions to them by looking at this sort of material online. People will spend hours of their time just as if they were going to real "porn" places ..... This can become more than a habit. Their lives can actually become unmanageable.

Back at the turn of the millennium Hustler magazine publisher Larry Flynt debated Rabbi Smhuley Boteach, author of the wildly popular "Kosher Sex", on the topic of Internet sex. Rabbi Boteach contends that it's destroying the male libido. There is ample clinical and testimonial proof to the Rabbi's assertion.

Real sex can become a letdown. Says Terry, an executive: The Internet has set unrealistic expectations. I now believe that my girlfriend is not as adventurous as I'd like. She's now very boring. I worry that cybersex may have skewed my reality of just how many people are running around having group.

It's a sentiment echoed by Neal,

The more you have sex with yourself, the more the experience becomes centered around your penis and nowhere else. I actually get a little annoyed if my partner tries to stimulate other parts of my body. The longer I do this, the worse I'm getting at real sex. The drive just isn't there.

Internet sex is - well - addictive. Take the case of Walter. He worked at home. Alone. He bought a PC for his home office and then he found IRC (Internet Relay Chat). 1,500 chat rooms filled to the rim with sex talk and pictures. When he got tired of trading pictures he moved up to Microsoft NetMeeting which sported real-time, movie-picture quality sex. He got hooked.

He started checking his sites constantly afraid he might miss something. Instead of working, he played the porn game - 6 to 8 hours a day. He also started to masturbate.

One of my clients told me a story about an employee at a satellite office she has in the state of Oregon. One day a second employee came up the stairs to find the door locked. When he opened it he could hear a laptop snap shut and George, the employee in question, fumbling with his pants.

Most men think that Internet sex is the greatest thing since sliced bread. That's because Internet sex gives men exactly what they want - sex without commitment or cost. Some have likened sex on the Net as hypnotic and timeless, with no pesky commercials to snap you back to reality. Viewing an endless stream of nudity and debauchery is like sitting in a windowless room with an unlimited supply of a powerful drug. Distinctions between day and night become irrelevant.

Alvin Cooper, Ph.D, a sex researcher, analyzed a group of more than 9,000 people who visited adult sites. He found that nearly 9 percent spent from 11 to 80 hours a week searching for online sex. For these people, Internet sex had become a compulsion.

It can develop more quickly, and it can also be much more powerful and more destructive. I saw a man a couple of weeks ago who had been looking at Playboy magazines .. .it had never been much of a problem ... But once he got on a computer, he was online with sexual materials for about six hours a day. You can imagine how six hours a day would have a tremendous negative effect on his life, on his relationships and on his work. He was online at work and at home. He couldn't stop. It was very powerful, very gratifying and immediate.

Dr. Cooper talks about the Triple A engine of the Internet

access, affordability and anonymity. And it's just this Triple A effect that has driven women onto the web in search of stimulation as well as men.

Tracy is a divorced mother of two who lives in Portland, Oregon. She entered a singles chat room and got hooked. Soon she was skipping meals and staying up late at night to chat with her new male friends. She began missing work, forgot her kids and rapidly lost all her inhibitions. She progressed from chats to cybersex to phone sex with 40 different men.

Dr. Cooper's study found that the Internet is an equalizer around sexuality for women. He found that women go online and experiment comfortable in their anonymity. Unfortunately, the study also found that women going online seem to develop sexual compulsivity at a similar rate to men online.

Aside from psychological addiction, an Internet sex habit can leave you in real psychic pain.

... must, get better. Can't, tell where, it's coming, from. Much struggle. Not happy. Headache. Backache. Eyes crossed. Stress, depression.

It can also destroy your relationships,

I am so happy to finally be out of this stupid relationship. 5 years of coping with someone's sexual addiction - coping or trying to cope with the guilt of knowing he is doing it to teens - and then not being able to have sex because he grosses you out so much.

Then there are the sexually transmitted diseases. A study appearing in the Journal of the American Medical Association found that people who use the Internet to find real-life sex partners are more likely to have had sexually transmitted diseases or engaged in risky intimated behavior. A JAMA editorial said that the findings weren't surprising, since the anonymity of sex facilitated by the Internet would be expected to appeal to sexual adventurers willing to take risks.

However you look at it, it's an huge industry. More than a quarter of Britons using the Internet from home visit pornographic websites. The NetValue survey, done during an average month, found that 3,879 of the 9,411 web sites visited were pornographic with Britons spending around 45 minutes a month looking at adult material. The worst offenders were students who account for nearly a quarter of all visits to pornographic sites.

Says 14-year old Brian from Maryland,

Finding porn on the Web is easier than researching for a homework assignment. What kid can't type in "porn. com? It's constantly being blasted at us from all directions. Venture into a chat room, and undoubtedly the junk mail will begin to flow. In recent months, unsolicited Instant Messages .... frequently pop up on my screen, advertising various pornographic Web sites. All I know is that when one of those unsolicited messages appears and the Web site accidentally load, along with it comes a massive burst of pop-up ads offering more, more. more.

That massive burst of pop-up ads is a rather nasty marketing technique whereby one web site automatically spawns another which automatically spawns another and so on. Eventually you have so many dirty web sites showing on your desktop that it's easier to just turn the damn thing off rather than to take the trouble of closing each one.

Most of the sites I stumble upon are porn sites. For instance, I was looking for pictures of elephants for my aunt and I stumbled upon pictures of women having sex with animals, not a pretty picture ... Today I was looking for a good teen Web site. I typed in www.teenscene.com. To my surprise it was a porn site. It's terrible how people are using the names of things young people might want to see and it comes out to be something perverted. .I believe that the government should ban these porn sites all together ... The minds of many young people are destroyed very frequently by this. I think that those who have "perverted" minds should not be ruining the ones of others.

15-year old Gio of Miami doesn't realize that porn is big business although he does have a point. Just why is it that you can see so many "free" hard-core images? While I'm not in favor of limiting anyone's First Amendment rights, the technology is most certainly there is create an Internet environment that would be palatable to all Internet users. One way to do this would be to limit the adult sites to an .sex domain name. Much like today's cable boxes where adult content can be blocked by concerned parents, an .sex domain name can be easily blocked by the software - and possibly even the hardware - in the future.

We don't seem to have the fortitude to go after the adult businesses, possibly because it's become so pervasive and too much money is changing hands.

As I write this another recession (shades of 2008) just might be looming. Scared by lost jobs and decimated pensions, folks are looking for a quick fix to the cash flow problem. For just a mere $49 they can get all the information they need to do this.

From and old New York Learning Annex catalog,

Did you know the adult Internet industry is a multi-billion dollar industry that makes up to 75% of all money generated on the Net? People are making a lot of money with adult sites - and so can you.

In this fun, interactive site, Jay Servidio, owner/president of teleteria.com, the largest provider of adult sites in North America, will reveal everything you'll need to know to start your business and make great profits.

67-year old retired schoolteacher Jean Winslow is someone who might have taken Servidio's course. She and a friend sell adult videos and marital "education" shows on the Internet. Says Winslow, "There's money to be made". She was one of 5,000 people who attended the ia2000 trade show in Las

Vegas. They came to strike deals, buy the latest technology and meet and greet - not unlike other Vegas trade shows such as Comdex.

Porn is a global, estimated $97 billion industry, with about $12 billion of that coming from the U.S, according to an NBC News report. In 2018 alone, more than ,517,000,000 hours of porn were consumed on the world's largest porn site. Sadly, Porn sites receive more regular traffic than Netflix, Amazon, & Twitter combined each month.

Given the economics of the Internet, more and more web-hosting firms and bandwidth sellers have to lean on porn purveyors. The infrastructure that we all use to get our e-mail and host our little family web sites then is being subsidized by Big Porn.

Hosting companies' massive data centers are the core of the Internet. They are also the brains of the porn industry. Data by PC Data Online and cross-references with NetCraft show that 13 out of the top 20 adult web sites are hosted by just a handful of large, well known public companies.

In spite of these reported statistics, it's really rather hard to figure out just who's making what. The Online Journalism Review says that most of the traditional media are just perpetuating myths about the porn industry. Gus Mastrapa, who is the entertainment editor of Hustler magazine, thinks that sales are not as high as the industry claims. He says that the porn industry is just following the lead of Hollywood, which exaggerates budgets of films as well as the film's grosses. He says the industry calls it creative accounting. Veteran porn personality Bill Margold puts it even more eloquently, "In an industry predicated on screwing, you're going to get f*****. You honestly expect us to tell you the truth about what we're making?"

Danni Ashe - she of the large assets - decided to create

her own website in 1995 to show off these assets. Little did she know that her 42-employee company would turn a $7 million profit just a few years later. Some companies have even gone public. Securities and Exchange Commission documents show that more than 15% of one notable company's stock is owned by institutional investors including the Oppenheimer and Vanguard mutual fund families. So if you've got some money tied up in some mutual funds, who knows, you might very well be a porn czar.

In a CBS.MarketWatch.com poll, only 17% admitted to ever having visited an adult web site. Compare this to the 75% Dr. Cooper found in his study. What accounts for the difference?

For one thing the Cooper study was done online and the MarketWatch study done live proving how easy it is to lie on the Internet. The Cooper study also found that 61 % said that they pretended to be a different age than they actually were; 5 percent pretended to be a different sex and 14 percent modified their attributes at whim.

Remember the tale of Cyrano de Bergerac? Cyrano did a great favor for a tongue-tied friend by penning love letters in his friend's name. Neither Cyrano nor his friend were quite what they appeared to be.

The Internet permits us to be whomever we wish to be. If you're 50 you can masquerade as 30. If you're a man, you can play at being a woman. If you're a child you can pretend to be an adult.

The Internet also makes us a lot braver than we are in real life. Most of us would never say or do in real life what we do regularly online. Something that happened to my niece is a good example. My nephew owns a bar so he asked his sister, my niece, to send out e-mails about an upcoming singles event to a list of e-mail addresses he had accumulated at the bar. My niece did as asked but instead of changing the "From" address to the name of the bar she left her own name. One young fellow, seeing this e-mail from a girl, decided to reply to the email requesting a date. The e-mail contained one extra added attraction - a nude photo of my niece's new suitor.

"Personal attribute enhancement" and unjustified bravado are really in bloom on the hundreds of dating service web sites. On match.com, Lori_71 is telling an obvious lie when she says that she loves both baseball and football. Dating services do sometimes work out. One of my students met her husband through a Christian dating service and she's been happily married for several years now.

Relationships do have a way of getting skewered because of the Internet. A distant cousin tells the story of her brother, who lost his wife to someone she met in an Internet chat room. Sight unseen, she packed up the car and drove North to Canada never to again return to her husband.

Sight unseen is usually a pretty bad idea. There was an Ally McBeal episode (popular GenX television series) where a woman developed a relationship with a wonderful man online. They decided not to exchange photographs. Instead, she also packed up her belongings and moved to Boston. The problem was that her new fiancé was a midget, leading us to the obvious conclusion that it's always wise to get a photograph first and fall in love later.

Photographs can lie, however. In one of my travels on the Internet, I came across a site that offered this bit of advice to protect against trans genders or transsexuals posing as cis women ask for a photograph that shows the person fully clothed. While it's easy to produce a fake photo of a naked woman, it's almost impossible to get a second photo with clothes on. If you get both, then chances are you have found yourself a real woman.

So, let's say you meet your perfect someone either online

or off. You've been dating for eight or so months but now the blush is off the rose. You try to break it off but the other person gets psycho and makes your life a living hell.

How can you get back at that person?

Mark created a web site to do just this after his girlfriend left him 50 "psychotic" voicemails in a very short period of time. The site, psychoexgirlfriend.com, which is now defunct, contained all of these voice mails as well as the now ubiquitous message board where psychoexgirlfriend and psychoexboyfriends can vent their spleen. Here's what hardpartypsychoex, all now defunct, had to say about her ex,

You know at first I was SEVERELY pissed that this ... idiot is once again splashing my life and pains all over the net. But this is actually quite comical. Going back & reading the email of mine he posted here, I see it only makes HIM not ME look like a freakin nut case. He is soo jealous of what I have now, cuz ne knows I'm happy and he knows he didn't make me happy. EVERYONE leaves him, cuz he is a LOSER!!!!!!!!!!!

If you really have no scruples, or are a bit young and dumb, you create a web site and post the sexual exploits of all your classmates. That's what two Chappaqua boys did to dozens of their female classmates. If Chappaqua sounds familiar to you it's because it is now the home of ex-President Bill Clinton. I guess his influence is really rubbing off on the community.

Fortunately, quite a few countries and municipalities have passed laws against this sort of revenge porn, including the UK, Canada and most of the 50 US states.

The Internet can also be a positive force where sex is concerned. According to Dr. Cooper, the Internet may be the best way for people to meet that has emerged in the past 20 years. Cooper says that the Internet provides a safe place to meet someone. It also forces people to talk and get to know each other.

One of the most powerful features of the Internet is that you can find a community to call your own. John runs a gay web site that specializes in foot fetishes,

The Internet has revolutionized erotic networking in several ways. People can gravitate towards areas that appeal to them personally and start building communities around like interests. For instance foot fetishism, (like most variations in sexuality) is stigmatized by the public (even within the gay population). For those with these desires there are very few safe venues through which they can pursue them. Prior to the Internet various erotic publications were the only resource. It often took weeks to implement meeting people through their personal classified ads, and mail correspondence takes too long. For someone into feet pouring over these personal ads in the hopes of finding someone else was the only option. Today, thanks to search engines, they simply enter "foot fetish" and are inundated with resources, created by like minded individuals with whom they can pursue/explore their common interests. No shame, no fear, and the opportunity to finally dialogue with others is affirming, empowering and really sexy. Also in this post-AIDS era, any form of safe and consensual alternative sex should be encouraged. Thankfully the Internet has made this possible.

When asked whether he thought pursuing relationships online had transformed the nature of traditional relationships, he answered,

I think this is totally relative, and depends on the preexisting dynamics between the couple in question. The Internet has led to many relationships, so improved communications can be good for people seeking companionship. I see the availability of sexual material on-line as a good thing in the big picture. America is still grappling with the scope of sexuality, and the Internet as helping us come to terms with this. Through exposure and dialogue we will get past our collective squeamishness regarding sex/ sexuality, and slowly pull out of this national adolescence. I see this as a paradigm shift that will impact the individual and the culture at large. If people are more comfortable with the sexual spectrum then perhaps relationships won 't be so rigid. Perhaps monogamy will be redefined as more of an emotional! spiritual commitment, and sex will be accepted more as a social! recreational force. Not that couples will stop having sex, but this kind of exposure might help destigmatize sexuality and make it less threatening.

The common thread through most of this book is that the Internet provides a great forum for communication between one or more people. In this chapter, we have been focusing on sex. But sex is more than just an act between two consenting adults. There are many gender issues wrapped up around this particular topic.

One of these issues is the choice to have sex but to remain childless - called childfree among those practicing the art form. It appears to be a popular lifestyle choice which has spawned its own Facebook group. Another of the childfree oriented sites is alt.support.childfree, a Google group, where one of its members posted this little missive,

If it's everyone's duty to look out for kids, then it's everyone's right to correct them when you won't. You can't subscribe to the "it takes a village" bit if you don 't want the villagers to complain when Junior is rude or destroys property ... Many of our parents are supportive of our of status. My mother is one of them. For that, I am grateful. I am also grateful that she taught me that having children is a CHOICE, and that you have no right to expect others to take on a responsibility that you CHOOSE to take on ...

Sharon Lopatka left her husband and her Maryland home to meet up with someone she knew had planned to kill her. Sharon met her killer on the Internet. E-mail messages from "Slowhand", the killer's nickname, described in detail how he was going to sexually torture and then kill her. She left her husband a note saying, "If my body is never retrieved, don't worry, know that I'm at peace".

While many Internet users were shocked at what happened, they felt there was a lot more to the story then the media or police were letting on or, perhaps, even knew. So 6 Tanith Tyrr used her prodigious skills as an Internet sleuth and habitue of alternative sex sites to find out a thing or two about Sharon and what happened to her,

Sharon Lopatka first met her killer in one of the numerous virtual townships that comprise the online community. She was a known poster in alt.sex.necrophilia, a Usenet newsgroup dedicated to discussing the subjects of sex and death, and an active participant in online adult chatting rooms. Using various "handles" or online identities -- Gina, Miranda, Vilado, Dion, Nancy and Sharon -- Lopatka actively solicited a man who would help her die. For a long time, she didn't have any luck, but she did find a number of people who shared her interest enough to talk about the subject with her online ..... Richard "met" Lopatka in cyberspace several times, in an online chat room forum. Often, they only talked, but in their first encounter they played out her fantasy. Richard briefly invented a scenario where he stabbed her with a knife, symbolically penetrating her, to which she reacted with sexual ecstasy rather than pain. They planned to meet again online, exchange photos and keep their correspondence going. But when she made it clear to him later on that she was interested in reality, not harmless fantasy, Richard balked.

My electronic research into the confusing tangle of Sharon Lopatka's various identities online uncovered some startling surprises. Apparently, she was one of the most disliked people on the Internet - a "spammer", an electronic vandal who places commercial advertising messages in massive volume in forums that are meant for chatting, not commercials .... Some of those advertisements were downright ludicrous. "I can cast a sex spell for YOU," one of her headlines blared, for an advertisement for a "warlock" offering to cast "love spells" for a fee .... Other businesses Lopatka was running included "Dion's Decorating Secrets " ... and her Classified Concepts advertising business. She also promoted several 1-900 phone numbers .... for which she collected revenue when people called.

The complete picture of Sharon Lopatka online reveals to my eye a woman who had serious problems in her life - and also one that lied to people online. Consequently, everything I learned from corresponding with her may well have been the elaborations of a habitual liar who was addicted to drama, a confession that she herself made at more than one point in online chat logs. From logs of activities in various chat rooms around the Internet, I discovered that Sharon claimed to some people that she had a close relative in Auchswitz, a German concentration camp. She stated that her family had made her miserable because she had "married a goy", and that she constantly felt guilty and persecuted. Her husband, she said, was difficult to live with and strongly resented her involvements online, to the point that she feared that he would physically destroy her computer. Interestingly enough, one advertisement from the Prodigy account for a job as a psychological counselor bears the name Victor Seton. Was this a pseudonym for her husband, or another scam Lopatka was running?

She also stated that she had been in trouble in the past for writing bad checks and for other fraud connected to her businesses, and that she had a deep wish to escape it all by dying. Apparently, she got her wish.

But was her final meeting with Glass a melodrama gone wrong? Did she believe that Glass, like everyone else she said she had talked to, would back off at the last moment and keep their erotic playa safe fantasy? Was Glass also operating under the assumption that their game was only a fantasy?

So it seems that you can be what you want to be on the Internet, even dead.

@SCAM

People lose their pets every day. Sometimes they tack posters onto utility poles or bus shelters offering an award for the return of their little furry friends. If they're lucky, a good Samaritan will find little Fluffy and return her safe and sound. If they're unlucky they'll get a call saying that Fluffy has been found and to drop off the money first and Fluffy will be returned later. Unfortunately, Fluffy never does arrive home.

The point of this story is that scams happen. And they happen all the time. We're all familiar with the old adage "a fool and his money is soon parted". It's true. And it's always been true.

I'm sure you've received one or a thousand sweepstakes entries from Publishers Clearing House. PCH sells magazine subscriptions and other paraphernalia. Their sales pitch comes in the form of a sweepstakes entry which, to the uninformed, looks like you need to purchase something to enter the sweepstakes.

One woman in her 70's spent $400 and $500 a month over five years on products purchased from sweepstakes companies. A woman in her 80's spent half of her Social Security check each month entering ..... A 78-year-old woman, so convinced she had won the big prize ... put a welcome sign for it in her front yard, *ordered a cake and was ready to celebrate her great fortune with friends.*

While the sweepstakes were indeed legitimate the wording of the message was the culprit. So much so that there were a variety of class action suits filed against well-known sweepstakes companies - and won. American Family Publisher,agreed to pay various states over a million dollars for violations of consumer laws. A $10 million dollar class action settlement was awarded to a group of sweepstakes-loving consumers who had been. Interestingly, out of the $10 million dollars attorney fees and other costs took away almost $6 million of that amount. But that's a scam of a different kind!

The point is that there are honest people and there are dishonest people. Usually the dishonest people try to take advantage of the honest people. Scams are as old as history. The Internet does add a whole new dimension to it, however.

I used to have faith in the American public. Now I'm not so sure. Why are so many people so gullible? I occasionally watch the Syfy channel and back in 2002 and 2003 saw a lot of commercials for a Miss Cleo, a telephone psychic, who has since passed away. Her first commercials were limited to the one cable channel and were pretty primitive. But soon, Miss Cleo was everywhere on cable and the production value of her commercials definitely improved. Apparently, Miss Cleo was doing a landslide business. She must have had many, many suckers - I mean clients.

Why do people believe in psychic hot lines? And why do they spend a big chunk of their paychecks on lottery tickets when the odds are millions to 1 that they'll win the jackpot? The reason is hope and desire to lead a better, more fulfilling life - usually with more money, the person of their dreams or both. In many instances, this desire for more money turns to downright greed as we'll see a bit later on.

The FBI says that thousands of people are victimized by online fraud schemes each year.

The old adage that you can't believe everything you read also holds true for what you read on the Internet.. .... criminals are aggressively exploiting the online world, where it's easy to attract consumers and hide identities.

The Federal Trade Commission is taking this seriously as well. They've built the Consumer Sentinel (1- 877-FTC-HELP), a web-based consumer complaint database. This database is not just consumer-driven. It is accessible and updateable. It receives data from a wide variety of other public and private consumer organizations including the Better Business Bureau, the FBI, the Department of Justice, all state Attorney Generals, the IRS as well as some foreign law enforcement organizations.

A bunch of these agencies got together recently in a rather prosaically named sweep of Internet scams. "Operation Top Ten Dot Cons" yielded 251 law enforcement actions. Once they sifted through the rubble they were able to figure out the top ten Internet cons,

Auction fraud
Internet Service Provider scams
Web site design/promotions also called "web cramming" Pyramid schemes
Business opportunities and work-at-home scams Investment schemes and get-rich-quick scams Travel! vacation fraud
Telephone / Pay-per-call solicitation frauds Health care frauds

One "con" not on the FTC list is most disturbing.

In California, a former security guard used the Internet to solicit the rape of a woman who rejected his advances .... The defendant terrorized his 28-year old victim by impersonating her in various Internet chat rooms and online bulletin boards, where he posted

along with her telephone number and address, messages that she fantasized being raped. On at least six occasions, sometimes in the middle of the night, men knocked on the woman's door saying they wanted to rape her.

When Jayne Hitchcock complained about a literary agency that appeared to be fraudulent she became a victim of cyberstalkers. Not only did they send her hundreds of e-mail messages, they posted forged messages in Internet discussion groups using her name. One of them went so far as to invite men to call or mail her their sexual fantasies to help her write a book. The email contained her real telephone and address.

I began receiving 25 to 30 phone calls a day from as far away as Germany … .It got so bad I had to see a psychotherapist to deal with my fears and paranoia.

After filing a $10 million dollar civil suit against three people connected to the literary agency, her lawyer received a death threat, neighbors received phone calls and complaints accusing her of stalking were filed with the Maryland attorney general's office, the FBI and Maryland state police.

Michael Lewis has a propensity for writing about the "brilliant" cyber-wild child. Lewis, a best-selling author and journalist, has written eloquently about Jonathan Lebed, a 15-year old investment wunderkid, and Marcus Arnold, a 15-year who convinced his cyber-chat mates that he was a top lawyer.

It totally amazed me when I read all the fawning articles about these two scammers. "So young and so brilliant" these articles say. Actually, these two young men do have much in common. Neither Marcus nor Jonathan had many friends and instead substituted the "friendship" of the Internet. More importantly, neither child was ever taught right from wrong. Even after the boys were "outed", their parents continued to beam proudly which must cause Dr. Spock turn over more than a few times in his grave.

15-year old Jonathan Lebed made close to a million dollars (you read that right) scamming unsuspecting (and ever-dumb) investment message board readers into bidding up stocks in which he invested.

One instance cited by the Securities and Exchange Commission involved Man Sang Holdings Inc. Little Johnny bought 18,000 shares of the stock on for between $1.37 and $20 a share. He then posted hundreds of messages indicating that the "stock was the most undervalued stock in history" and would soon hit $20 a share. More than one million Man Sang shares traded and the stock's price doubled. Lebed sold his shares and pocketed a profit of more than $34,000.

Some would argue, Peter Lewis the most vocal of them, that what Lebed did is no more wrong than what Morgan Stanley Dean Witter's Mary Meeker, a former well-known securities analyst, did for a living. Meeker got paid some $15 million a year to chat up stock prices. So why not prosecute Meeker and Merrill Lynch's Henry Blodget? Aren't the fund managers, analysts and other assorted stock-hawkers guilty of the same thing? Well yes, but that doesn't mean that everyone should get off scot-free. In fact, literally hundreds of lawsuits are regularly filed against a variety of investment houses, regulatory bodies and the investment houses themselves are implementing new rules. In the end the investment houses will pay a pretty penny for the error of their ways.

Pumping and dumping is wrong wherever it is done. That's common sense and the law. If you violate it, you better expect the Feds will come calling. When they do, you should stop your behavior or pay the price -- not get a magazine article about you in your defense that makes your opponents [the Feds] look like Keystone Knuckleheads. In the Lebed case the good guys won. Don't ever forget that.

While Lebed had to give back over a quarter million in allegedly ill-gotten gains the SEC inexplicably let him keep roughly $500,000 more. Apparently, the SEC didn't really want the notoriety of prosecuting a 15-year old. In addition, the SEC was itself culpable since it, until recently, failed to lay down stringent guidelines about what is or is not permissible.

Still, stock manipulation is illegal and it saddens me that people like Peter Lewis write glowing articles about him and that Lebed's father, instead of being mortified and apologetic, actually told reporters that he was proud of his son. Many parents, it would appear, are raising children to be scammers. The current college admission scandal is a testament to that!

While Jonathan Lebed had greed as his motivation, you can't say that for Marcus Arnold. This 15-year old also achieved notoriety by posting information on Internet message boards. In Arnold's case he anointed himself an experienced attorney and started answering legal questions posted to askme.com's legal bulletin board.

The philosophy behind askme.com, which shut its doors in 2016, and was to use technology to elicit knowledge from the unwashed, but possibly experienced, masses rather than just those "at the top" [read this those with education and credentials]. Actually, this philosophy really does have a sound basis within organizational theory. Most modern corporations are hierarchical in nature. There are few bosses and many subordinates. These organizations are structured such that those at the top of this pyramid are deemed experts who filter information down to the lowly masses - i.e. the rest of us. Sometime during the 1990s organizational theory gave birth to a new structure which was much flatter. Instead of a pyramid this structure looked more like a pancake where expertise could flow, not only from top to bottom, but from bottom to top. AskMe's software was created to facilitate this.

Somewhere along the way AskMe launched its public web site and therein lies the problem. Within an organization, even in a pancake-shaped one, there are checks and balances about the nature of expertise flowing throughout the organization. If Joe the mail boy comes up with a great idea the company indeed knows who Joe is. This is not exactly true about public message boards such as AskMe.com where folks hide behind screen names and anyone can take on any identify. Joe the mail boy can claim to be Joe the President and no one would even know. Even more unfortunate, few who use these message boards even ask

Arnold, unlike Lebed, didn't do what he did for the money. In fact, no money ever changed hands. Arnold more than likely did it for the attention and because he actually enjoyed the law. Like Lebed, Arnold wasn't one of the more popular kids in school. He also had lots of spare time and an Internet connection. There's an old fable about a bunch of monkeys in a room. In this tale each monkey was given a typewriter and all the monkeys proceeded to bang away at the keys. A few days later, when the door to the room was opened, the monkeys had neatly re-created text for Shakespeare's Hamlet. The moral of this story is that given enough time and the right equipment even the dumbest of the dumb can accomplish great things.

Now, I don't mean to imply that Lebed and Arnold were dumb. On the contrary, both appear to be clever boys. However, the media has a habit of jumping to unwarranted conclusions when adolescents do apparently "irnpossible" things with computers. Because many in the media are not particularly tech-savvy ordinary capabilities are often portrayed as a real demonstration of extraordinary intelligence. This is usually pretty far from the truth. For example, the media often describe teenage computer hackers with awe. In actuality, many teenage hackers are just copycats. Referred to as "script kiddies", these kids copy hacking programs from the Internet and then merely run them - hardly any genius here. So while Arnold and Lebed are certainly clever, they are by no means brilliant. They both had plenty of time and motivation.

Arnold's claim to fame on AskMe.com was his willingness to spend an inordinate amount of time answering simple legal questions posed by people imprudent enough to take legal advice from the equivalent of a stranger standing on a street corner.

Using a screen name of LawGuy1975 and carefully tailoring his profile to add a number of years to his age and much experience to his resume, Arnold was able to answer questions such as "What amount of money must a person steal or gain through fraud before it is considered a felony in Illinois" and "Can a parole officer prevent a parolee from marrying". Although Arnold claims never to have read a law book or use any legal web sites, he does admit to watching Court TV. It's hard to believe, however, that Court TV so conveniently provides all the answers that Arnold would need to answer questions specific to particular jurisdictions.

Though he lied about his background and age, astonishingly he does seem to have his defenders on the AskMe site.

These aren't hallowed halls and this isn't a law office. This board is the personification of the free market in information at work. There are no qualifications for being an expert on this board except one's own temerity to announce it to the world.

Caveat emptor!

It seems that some kids today are more vicious and much less honest than ever before - or at least it seems that way. One only has to pick up a newspaper to read of yet another seemingly sociopathic outrage. We all know by now about the Columbine, Sandy Hook and Stoneman Douglas massacres. Granted, these are extraordinary occurrences. But there are many more instances of this sort of behavior that never make the national news.

End of school usually is greeted with a resounding cheer. In Paterson, New Jersey, end of school was met with death. A dozen or so teenagers left school for the last time and proceeded to punch their way home. When they got to Hector Robles, a 43 year old homeless man, they punched and kicked him to death. Perhaps just as shocking as the crime was the reaction of the teens and their parents when the teens were finally brought in for justice.

What struck police later was how students who were brought in for questioning told the story of the spree in a calm manner - as if, perhaps, they were going to the mall. None expressed remorse, say police. Many seemed nonchalant.

In fact, after leaving Robles lifeless on the sidewalk, several of the teenagers reportedly went to a friend's house and spent the after swimming in a backyard pool. Most disturbingly, the teens' parents appeared just as heartless as their children, implying that the death of a homeless man should not get in the way of the future of their children.

So it's no wonder that teens are taking to the Internet in great numbers to do evil deeds usually without but sometimes with the blessing and active involvement of their parents.

In North Syracuse several high school seniors posed as a 23-year old woman and tried to lure a male teacher into engaging in "cybersex". Even worse they later tried to extort $50 each to keep quiet.

Over the course of several weeks these students sent instant messages to the teacher trying to entice the teacher into sending sexual messages back and forth. Finally, they enticed the unsuspecting teacher into a chat room where they revealed their identities. When the students threatened to distribute copies of their correspondence unless $50 was paid to each of them the teacher reported the incident to school officials. All three students were charged with attempted grand larceny and coercion.

The most popular places on the Internet are also the most risky place on the Internet. eBay offers online auction services. You can buy virtually anything at a Web auction - from cars to Barbie dolls. It has even been reported that some ghoulish person was hawking body parts until he was shut down.

When an Apple computer went on sale some poor schnook mailed a cashier's check for the full amount by priority mail. The thing of it was that police were already onto this scheme and laid a trap for the schemer.

Vancouver police Detective Ed Hewitt says that since the Internet was unleased thousands of victims worldwide have lost millions in these Internet-related schemes where expensive merchandise was bought and paid for but never delivered. Luckily for the schnook, Hewitt was on the ball and had notified check cashing services to be on the lookout for the perpetrator. The check was returned and the perp arrested so all's well in the world. Right?

Actually, the answer is no. In spite of all the publicity surrounding these high profile cases people continue to show their gullibility by believing mostly anything and everybody connected to the Internet. Although most auction web sites provide escrow services, people seem to be in such a rush to get their "bargain" that they throw all caution to the wind. Not long after our Vancouver fellow wound up in hot water, a 23-year old Oklahoman was arraigned on a 12-count federal indictment that accused him of defrauding people in nine states and the District of Columbia by not delivering the new "high-end" computers he had offered for sale online.

Pam Lanouette is a single mother of three who was down to her last couple of hundred dollars and Christmas was just around the corner when she placed an ad online asking if anyone had tickets to an upcoming concert. A man from South

Florida called and said that he did indeed have great 10th row tickets to the concert and she could get them by wiring $500 to him via a Money Gram. He said that once he got the money he'd ship her the tickets via overnight mail. Of course, the tickets never arrived and Lanouette was out her last $500 - to say nothing about how disappointed her three kids were. She says,

I always tell people if it sounds too good to be true, it probably is. If you don't know the person at the other end of the line. If they're just a name hiding out there in cyberworld then don't do the deal.

Of course, good advice is seldom taken - at least not by people looking to make a quick financial killing. Even before the introduction of the Internet, pyramid schemes were picking off the easy money using commercials and classified ads. Pyramid schemes really hit their stride when the Internet came along.

In December of 2000, the FTC settled a case with two people who had done exactly this and netted $435,000 before the FTC shut them down, These two entrepreneurs - the bilk-ors - charged a registration fee for a chance to "make money off the Internet". In return the bilk-ees received a kit instructing them to place the same kind of ads and charge the same fees. In another interesting case of an Internet-based pyramid scheme, Federal regulators stepped in to stop a scheme masquerading as an Internet investment club. In this one, Le Club Prive bilked some 2,000 investors out of $5.6 million. For a $1,495 membership fee plus $149 a month, Le Prive offered investors the chance to earn commissions by recruiting new members to the club. Members were promised access to the club's Internet backroom which supposedly contained investment recommendations and shares of domestic and offshore hot mutual funds.

Pyramid schemes are often likened to the stock market. Everyone knew that Amazon.com was bleeding red ink but they still plunked down $400 per share in hopes that the dream would last just long enough that they make their "killing" and then get out – in this case, they were right. In other words, the philosophy behind the stock market - and these pyramid schemes - is "screw the other guy".

The problem is that you're the one that generally gets screwed. I suppose there really is meaning to the old adage "turn about is fair play."

Sometimes it's best to travel in packs to make sure you're not scammed. Rod Allee, a journalist, had bid on a computer. Then he got an e-mail saying that he was a winner of the auction. Because this was for a lot of 15 computers there were other winners as well. After he got the e-mail he sent one of his own off to the seller asking him where to send the money and what arrangements would be made to guarantee that he did indeed receive the computer.

A few seconds later he got an e-mail from another auction winner,

Like you, I was a winning bidder. The seller e-mailed me to send him the money even though he unregistered from the Internet auction site. What do you think?

Then Allee got another e-mail from another "winner" indicating that a buyer from Boston had contacted the seller, discovered that he too lived in the Boston area, and had offered to pay for and pick up his computer in person. The seller refused. At this point e-mails started flying all over the place. One winner tried to reach the seller by phone only to find that there was no such listing.

In the end the fraud was foiled. These folks may not have really won an auction but they did beat out the scammer.

Sometimes even the good guys get scammed. Audi Lanford is co-editor of ScamBusters which is one of the most prominent of scambusting organizations.

What would you do if you got an e-mail thanking you for an $899 order you had never placed? And what if the return e-mail address bounced back to you as undeliverable? Would you call the customer complaint number which also appeared on the e-mail? You bet you would.

If you did, your next phone bill would have been whopping! The reason is that the listed complaint number went through to the West Indies and was then relayed to an adult entertainment pay service.

This is telephone fraud - Internet style - a scam which ScamBusters tackled over five years ago. Evidently a scammer found it most amusing to send out thousands of e-mails on ScamBusters letterhead warning of a "major scam" involving web surfers who have lost as much as $26,000 returning calls to 900 area code numbers.

How do Internet telephone scams usually work? There are a variety of interesting techniques but the most interesting is when you visit a web site or receive an email that asks you to download a program to better access its site. Most of us think nothing of honoring this request. We do it all the time for audio and video players. What these folks are asking you to download is a bit different however from what you're used to. Once the program is downloaded it typically breaks the Internet connection and then reconnects to the Web via an international long distance phone number at rates as high as $7 a minute. As long as the Internet connection is unbroken those $7 charges add up - even if you close your browser.

This is exactly what happened to Christine Ver Ploeg. She wound up with an $801.03 phone bill for repeated calls to the tiny island of Niue, just east of New Zealand. Ver Ploeg's computer made 11 calls to Niue lasting from one to 19 minutes between 3 and 5 a.m. Her family still doesn't know what triggered the calls but she still had to fight with her long-distance provider to get a refund.

John and Terri Nakai wanted another child very badly. They had been waiting for over a year with a local adoption agency when a fellow subscriber to an online service e-mailed them about the chance to adopt a baby almost immediately. After sending this scammer $4,500, the first installment of her $8,500 fee, the scammer was never heard from again. Sonya Furlow had duped the Nakais and 43 other families from California to Maine.

People are getting burned on the Internet at a rate that is inconceivable, says Bill Pierce, a founder of the National Council for Adoption. Electronic chat rooms are trolled by scammers promising babies if only the adopters will send money.

There are other scams that prey on people's vulnerabilities. Many people believe that alternative therapies can cure whatever ails them. Many marketers use web sites and e-mail to prey on the sickest and most vulnerable consumers. Scammers market a variety of devices to cure cancer, AIDS/HIV, arthritis, hepatitis, Alzheimer's, diabetes and many other diseases.

Some of these web sites and e-mail made unusual and unfounded claims, people could cancel their surgery, radiation or chemotherapy in favor of herbal cures that cost hundreds of dollars; a device that delivered mild electric current would kill the parasites that cause such serious diseases as cancer and Alzheimer's; and that those with HIV or AIDS could use St. John's Wort as a safe treatment for the disease.

Many of the web sites are jeopardizing the health and safety of consumers with outlandish promises and false hopes. Unfortunately, examples of questionable products being peddled on the Web abound .... The Internet provides many benefits. But, its unique qualities - including its broad reach, relative anonymity, and ease of creating new websites or removing old ones - pose new enforcement challenges.

One of the companies the FTC went after was Arkansas-based FoxMor, Inc. Among other things, FoxMor claimed that the ingestion of colloidal silver is proven effective in treating over 650 infectious diseases including cancer, diabetes, leprosy, lupus and malaria and that medical tests prove that ingestion is safe and has no adverse side affects.

These claims were, of course, unfounded. Neither FoxMor nor anyone else, without significant medical studies, can prove that colloidal silver does everything that it's touted to be able to do.

FoxMor and its brethren were actually given an out by the FTC decision. All the decision said was that FoxMor could no longer make the claims that it was making for colloidal silver. The decision didn't say that FoxMor couldn't sell it. The market that it has migrated to, in fact, is even more lucrative than its original market. According to Donald Leggett of the FDA,

Some surfing should clearly demonstrate that such promotions are increasing. The purveyors continue to "outsmart" consumers. Many of these consumers do not trust the "authorities" and / or simply wish to decide for themselves.

Many educated and usually cautious people believe the claims of the "new age" health supplements market. Indeed, some of these supplements have been used for years in Europe, China and among native populations in exotic far-away places. Some of these supplements undoubtedly do work, but personally, I have no level of comfort in treating my own body as a lab rat and trying these things out.

The dietary supplement market is largely unregulated and a wild west market it is. Anything goes here giving new meaning to caveat emptor - except in this case you just might be caveat-ing with your life.

Of course, you run the risk of complications when taking medically approved drugs as well. Fen-Phen is a good example of this.

When fen-phen hit the market in 1996, it was labeled a "miracle cure" for weight loss. Ultimately, it was found that fen-phen caused serious medical side effects including Primary Pulmonary Hypertension - and was withdrawn from the American market in July of 1997 leaving a trail of litigation in its wake.

The differences between the dietary supplement market and the traditional medical market can be read between the lines of the short account of fen-phen I provided above. Medically approved drugs are continually being tested and re-tested and when problems are found are quickly recalled. The dietary supplement market is largely unregulated, untested, not given to recalls and, hence, much more risky.

We've already talked about Jonathan Lebed, the 15-year wunderkid with greed on the brain. His notoriety was not because of his deed but because of his age. There are plenty of older folks who also have greed on the brain, access to the Internet and a penchant for investment fraud - and it's not just limited to the United States.

Four million folks received an e- that seemed to good to be true. Shares in Rentech, a NASDAQ listed company, were about to go through the roof. Even more found out about Rentech through postings on various investment bulletin boards. Indeed, the price of Rentech did double on the very next trading day. But this, of course, was just a scam.

Two Aussies devised a clever scheme. Steven Hourmouzis bought 65,500 Rentech shares just a few days before he and his partner, Wayne Loughnan, did their dirty deed. The two actually thought that they had devised a brilliant scheme. They would not send the spam from their own e-mail address - spammers never do. Instead, they would "break and enter" into the mail servers of legitimate organizations and send their spam from there. The companies comprised included SAAB,

Tasmania Department of Health and the Lost Dog's Home.

But the boys tripped up. The Australian Securities and Investments Commission, which is equivalent of the US Securities and Exchange Commission, put the bloodhounds on the case. They reported,

As people use the Internet they leave electronic footprints with service providers, telecommunications carriers and internet service providers, said Keith Inman, Director of Electronic Enforcement at ASIC. These footprints can be painstakingly reconstructed from computer records of the transactions. We were able to trace the identity of the suspects by following the electronic trail left by postings on the bulletin boards and their spam e-mails.

ASIC, like me, believes that at least one sucker is born every minute. They set out to prove this. ASIC placed a banner advertisement with Yahoo which directed suckers - em - surfers to a fake web site offering fantastic returns. ASIC called their bogus firm, Millennium Bug Insurance. The site claimed that MBI would be able to charge high premiums, giving investors a great rate of return.

This bogus site received more than 10,000 hits during April. More than 1,200 people asked for further information, and 233 people pledged either $10,000 or $50,000 of their hard-earned money. More than $4.2 million was offered to MBI even through information provided on the web site was unsubstantiated, there was no prospectus, no license to offer an investment and the investments were not offered by a public company. Unbelievable, isn't it? As the former Chairman of ASIC, Alan Cameron, puts it,

This shows how willing people are to part with large sums of money without finding out anything about the company they are giving their money to. Some people, who might normally question the validity of an investment offer, seem to think that offers on the Internet come with some authority. They don't! Taking advice *over the Internet is the same as taking advice from someone on a street corner. Handing over $50,000 on the Internet is the same as handing over $50,000 to someone on the street.*

In the end trust no one.

I don't want to rain on anyone's parade but the world is a mean place. The Internet can be even meaner.

At night Abraham Abdallah was a mere dishwasher in a New York restaurant. By day, however, he used the Internet to access the financial details of the Fortune 500, including Steven Spielberg, and then redirected cash from their accounts into the fraudulent accounts he had set up. With the help of forged corporate notepaper, some rubber stamps and information scooped up from the Internet, Abdallah and an accomplice were able to clone the identities of these famous folks and siphon away some big bucks.

A similar scam with even more cash involved was foiled in Europe. In this case $3.9 billion - that's right, billion - of forged bank and financial institution guarantees was published to 29 different web sites with the purpose of luring potential clients to invest in projects and finance schemes.

When Lee Schamens, president of Badger Blueprint, received a $62,000 Internet order for ink jet cartridges he was ecstatic. Luckily, Schamens is one smart CEO because he decided that something just didn't smell right. The first red flag was that the purchaser wanted the shipment to go to the African republic of Benin. The second red flag was that the check was drawn from a Texas hospital's bank account. Turns out the check was stolen, altered via computer and then sent to Badger.

Possibly the very worst thing that can happen to anyone is identity fraud. This happens when someone gets a hold of your personal information and then essentially clones you. The cloned you takes out credit, buys things and then skips town. You're left holding the bag.

Joseph Michael Hoban was very clever. He solicited people over the phone to write checks to charities and health causes such as for muscular dystrophy patients. He didn't bother to cash their checks, however. Instead he used the information to apply for and get credit cards and steal from his victim's bank accounts. Another of his scams was to advertise phony nursing positions on the web. He then used information from a job applicant to open a credit card account in her name.

I'd like to close this chapter with an e-mail that I've gotten pretty regularly over the past couple of years. Read it for yourself. If you're ready to do business with these folks I'd like you to do one thing first - re-read this chapter.

ALHAJI ADAMU SHAGARL Lagos, Nigeria
FAX NO: 234 1 7594693

Private   Address:alh   adamushagari@presidency.com   alh adamushagari@justice.com

ATTN.: THE MANAGING DIRECTOR / C. E. O.

REQUEST FOR URGENT (CONFIDENTIAL BUSINESS RELATIONSHIP OF THE TRANSFER OF US$45,560,000. 00 (FORTY FIVE MILLION, FIVE HUNDRED AND SIXTY THOUSAND UNITED STATES DOLLARS ONLY).

I hope this letter will not embarrass you since we have not had any previous communication. I got your reference from the United States (your country) trade department under private enquiry that is not related to my aim of writing you this letter and went further to have it confirmed by the Nigeria Exports Promotion Council

(NEPC).

1, on behalf of my other colleagues from different Federal Government of Nigeria owned parastatals decided to solicit your assistance as regards the transfer of the above stated amount into your bank account. This fund arose from the over-invoicing of various contracts awarded in my parastatals to certain foreign contractors some time ago.

We as holders of official positions in various parastatals, were mandated by this new civilian government to scrutinize all payments made to certain foreign contractors by the past Military Government and we discovered that some of the contracts they executed were grossly over invoiced, either by omission or commission. Also we discovered that the sum of $65,560,000.00 (Sixty-Five Million, Five Hundred and Sixty Thousand United States Dollars Only) was lying in a suspense account, although the foreign contractors were fully paid their entitlements after executing the said contracts. We all agreed that the over-invoiced amount be transferred (for our own use) into a bank account provided by a foreign partner, as the code of conduct of the Federal Civil Service does not allow us to operate foreign accounts.

However, we have succeeded in transferring some of these money, precisely US$20, 000, 000. 00 (Twenty Million United States Dollars Only) into a foreign account in GENEVA (SWITZERLAND). But unfortunately, the provider of the account has severed all forms of contacts with us as he has refused to adhere to our earlier mutual agreement insisting that the total amount be paid into his nominated bank account before disbursement will take effect. If for US$20M (Twenty Million United States Dollars Only) we are not compensated, how can one guarantee full compensation on remittance of the balance of US$45.560M (Forty-Five Million, Five Hundred and Sixty Thousand United States Dollars Only).

We are therefore seeking your assistance based on the balance amount of US$45.560M, which can be speedily processed and fully remitted into your nominated bank account. On successful remittance of the fund into your account, you will be compensated with 25% of the amount for assistance and services and 5% set aside for expenses contingency.

This transaction is closely knitted and in view of our SENSITIVE POSITION we cannot afford a slip, I assure you that this transaction is 100% risk free. We will avail you with our identities as regards our respective offices, when relationship is fully established and

smooth operation commences. I am at your disposition to entertain any question(s) from you in respect of this transaction, so contact me immediately through the above and fax number or through my direct email address
alh *adamushagari@presidency.comor*
alh *adamushagari@justice.comfor further information on the requirements and procedure. Please note that the DEAL needs utmost confidentiality and your immediate response will be highly appreciated and we will use our own share of the money to establish a lucrative business in your country. Please you should contact me immediately with your private fax and telephone numbers where further details in respect to this transaction would be sent to. Please do not disregard my email for any reason because it was addressed to and from myself, it is for security reason to avoid problem.*

Yours truly,

ALHAJI ADAMU SHAGARI.

@HATE

The fossil record tells us that over the past 4 million years, multiple species of hominid typically shared Earth's environment. Being alone in the world as a species, as we are today, is the exception, not the rule. The only obvious reason for the current state of affairs is that Homo sapiens is an unusual creature, intolerant of competition by close relatives and able to do something able it.

When Homo Sapiens arrived in Europe the Neanderthals were already there. Within 10,000 years the Neanderthals had disappeared off the face of the earth, except for a wee trace found in our DNA. There is much conjecture about the reasons for their disappearance. One theory holds that they simply but peaceably failed in competition with their smarter, more creative Homo sapiens cousins. Another, more radical, theory is that Homo Sapiens simply annihilated their slower, less talented cousins. We have a real history, it appears, of just not getting along with each other.

Most people, in spite of "politically correct" protestations to the contrary, are tribal. Their preference is to be with people of their own race, color, and/or religion.

Picture a world in the next century organized not around nation-states but around a new form of tribes sharing the same culture and values. It's a world where you pledge allegiance not to a republic, but to a clan.

So says Peter Leyden in the Dark Side. He goes on to describe the state of our fracturing world and the fact that the melting-pot business is not working out. He says that America no longer seems able to meld all the various peoples within its borders into one harmonious whole,

As the years go by, Americans seems to identify less with their nation and more with their various subgroups based on ethnicity, religion or race.

The rest of the world is simmering with the same tensions. The Soviet Union, Yugoslavia and even Canada have all either splintered or are in danger of doing so. Not surprisingly, the Internet can aid and abet this process of "fractionation". The Internet allows people to connect with people more like themselves to the exclusion of others different from them. On the other hand, the Internet affords unlimited potential for people to connect with people quite unlike themselves. It all depends on the path a particular person chooses. And when even the President of the United States sows divisions via tweet, it can be lamented that all is lost.

sucks.com (now defunct and taken over by, I don't know what) - pardon my bad language – was created as a web site for whiners. It described itself as a place where all people can get together and vent their grievances about corporate America, American politics and politicians. The "sucker" with the most votes seems to be the United States itself. But on this particular message board it wasn't Americans who were whining about America, it was people who don't even live here,

.... the US was formed when European countries send all their jail population to the "New World" .... so kind of in two hundred twenty five years the roots of US citizens does not evolve to a love/caring and understanding peoples .... why the US have the biggest criminality rate? Anyhow .... doesn't matter .... US really SUCKS .... may be not

you or some other US citizen .... but the majority ..... SUCKS ....

And an American rose to the occasion,

... Not too many years ago you would not have been allowed access to the internet. Think your Soviet masters would have allowed any sort of communication to be posted to a public forum called RomaniaSucks or USSRsucks or CommunistsSuck?

It's a well-known fact that the United States is hated far and wide as is evident in this posting. Why is that? Pre-Trump, part of the reason was simply America's success and its rather high standard of living compared to the rest of the world. People will always envy other people and oftentimes that envy turns into rage and ultimately into hate.

Another emotion that frequently morphs into hate is fear. We generally fear that which we do not understand - those Asians that moved in next door or those African-Americans living across town.

In the past six weeks, rioting has hit the towns of Oldham and Burnley [United Kingdom] - like Bradford, working class northern communities with large Asian populations, mainly people whose roots lie in the Indian subcontinent.

Perhaps the greatest cause of tribal tension, at least in the United States, is affirmative action programs. These, though well-intentioned, have pitted citizen against citizen and neighbor against neighbor for a piece of, what is perceived to be, an ever-diminishing pie consisting of the right job, the right university and the right governmental opportunity.

The Supreme Court has not ruled on the question of race as a university admissions factor since its 1978 decision in University of California Regents v. Bakke. Then, a five justice majority struck down a medical school's policy of setting aside a fixed percentage of slots for minorities. Four justices voted to uphold the program, saying it was needed to compensate for past discrimination.

In the Bakke case a high-scoring Caucasian was denied admission to law school in favor of a lower-scoring African-American. The case touched a raw nerve among many Americans back in the late seventies with the bad feeling continuing and even escalating decades later.

The anger, for the most part, has been muted by the forces of multi-culturalism and political correctness. Disagree with diversity and you are labeled a racist, particularly by the liberal press. Even the most benign of arguments, if it concerns minorities, takes on a racist cast if uttered by a "majority."

Many communities around the country have been besieged by armies of illegal aliens who gather weekday mornings on selected curbsides awaiting day work in lawn maintenance and construction. The men loiter, avail themselves of nearby bushes to relieve themselves, and occasionally make the typical male noises to passing females. Nearby single family homes have been reconfigured to create rooming houses for sometimes up to twenty men at a time. Yet when neighbors complain they are called bigots, either directly or indirectly, by pro-immigration advocates.

While numerous pro-immigrant groups, both national and local, work to protect the rights of immigrants, the Sachem Quality of Life Organization has provided, for the past four years, a less familiar and more controversial point of view. Its mission is to stand up for the rights of middle-class suburban communities it says are being inundated by thousands of undocumented, mostly Latino, immigrants. The NY Times had this to say about Sachem,

But the forum is raising new questions about whether it will be a legitimate gathering for discussion and advocacy of issues relating to immigration or an angry one aimed at further stigmatizing those at the bottom of the socioeconomic pecking order.

Now the NY Times article does not out and out accuse

the Sachem group of bigotry but the statement above is very clear albeit very subtle.

For forty years the black-white issue has gone unresolved. Into the mix has also crept the rising tide of immigration which brought to our shores (and the shores of our European cousins) millions of people unlike those that were already here and, perhaps more importantly, entirely unlike each other.

This is the fractionation that the Leyden article alludes to. Today many towns and cities appear to be carved up into informal ethno-districts. In New York City, Flushing has become so predominately Asian that its store signs are no longer in English.

The rage lives on, however. Once undercover because it was the topic that the media would seldom cover, the Internet has brought it to the forefront. At the turn of the century,

When it was announced that Senator Joseph Lieberman was Al Gore's choice for running mate the Internet was deluged with hate mail, racial slurs and examples of the intolerance that lies beneath the surface of American society. Press reports claimed half or more of the postings on the Lieberman choice included offensive remarks about Lieberman and Jews in general.

At the time, AOL (America Online), which recorded more than 28,000 postings on Lieberman actually had to delete an unspecified number for violating its policies against hate speech. CBS suspended 10 users from its chat rooms.

Public message boards are a breeding ground for just such intolerance. Facebook, Reddit and others play host to a wide variety of public forums. A member of the South River Board of Education posted a series of Facebook posts criticizing Muslims and Islam.

MSNBC has named the world's top ten most dangerous cities. They are all under Islamic control. Funny thing, that religion of love, just saying," he posted in 2011. That same year he posted Another reason why I hate the religion of love (referring to Islam.)"

Even well-intended message boards sometimes go awry. One such board was the former Lycos Communities' Cultures and Ethnicity Board where the topic of white bigotry was heatedly debated.

And what do you mean "join the human race". We are the human race. White does not make you better or worse.

And sometimes bigotry gets even more specific as when this poster posted a thread called "white bigotry especially among women."

I believe the female is the most evil of all species .... Evil doesn't even come close to describing the female species. They are self-centered, egotistical, backstabbing, unloyal, cruel, heartless, hateful, manipulating, untrustworthy, mouthy, vengeful, unenlightened pieces of walking human refuse.

Ouch! This last poster most definitely had use of a good Thesaurus. Unfortunately, the animus towards women has only increased over the years. The self-describes incel (involuntarily celibate) has multiple discussion groups just dripping in hate. Sadly, as a result, there have been several mass shootings as a result.

Backstabbing women are the least of the Internet's problems with hate speech. There are far worse sites lurking in the ether.

Stormfront markets itself as a purveyor of "white pride worldwide". This is the site created by Don Black, a former leader of the Ku Klux Klan. His contention is that the web is the most important thing to happen to extreme politics in years.

...whereas we previously could only reach people with our pamphlets, or by holding rallies with no more than a few hundred people, now we can reach potentially millions of people.

In 1998 Black was interviewed on ABC News Nightline, along with Rabbi Abraham Cooper of the Simon Wiesenthal Center, an organization that monitors hate groups. In this dialog Black testifies to the fact that the Internet has provided his group with the opportunity to bring their point of view to hundreds of thousands of people who would never have otherwise subscribed to one of their publication or been in touch with one of their organizations. This is exactly what frightens Rabbi Cooper,

The lunatic fringe has embraced this technology with a sophistication and a veracity that is frightening .... What started as a trickle has now evolved into an incredible deluge. In the last year alone, we've seen s 300 percent increase in the number of these pages that have been put up on the world wide web. So literally everyone is jumping in and it's not just groups here in the United States and it 's not just traditional racists and bigots. There are anarchists thrown in. There are individuals whose orientation or concerns we're not even sure of.

Stormfront, and the thousands like it, are politically extreme. They promote hate, white supremacy and race war, and see anti-government terrorists such as Timothy McVeigh as the icons of their movement.

A tour though some of these sites is eye-opening. On the Stormfront message boards there is a study in denial and revisionism,

The Jews with their elegant museums, spreading across America and Europe like poisonous mushrooms never offer physical evidence of this horrible accusation against my people and my culture .... 55 years after this alleged Holocaust, there is not ONE shred of physical evidence or wartime document that corroborates the existence of these mystical gas chambers.

This same site also does a brisk business in confederate flags and other "white pride" paraphernalia. Nazi paraphernalia is also a hot seller on the web. Yahoo got into trouble by hosting online auctions of Nazi paraphernalia. In November of 2000 a French court ruled that Yahoo bar French users from viewing all Nazi-related auctions and "any other site that may be construed as an apology for Nazism."

Don't think that hate sites originate from hate hardened older individuals like the KKK's Don Black, there are more than just a few teen-based hate sites. Part of the problem might be teenage proclivity for always doing the wrong thing. A survey, conducted by Websense, Inc. and Yankelovich Partners, found that 58 percent of teens have accessed an objectionable website; 39 percent have seen sites featuring offensive music; 25 percent have seen sites featuring sexual content; and 20 percent have seen sites featuring violence.

A bunch of Marlboro, New Jersey middle-schoolers created a website filled with threats against teachers and students. The "Marlboro Middle School's Mafia Web Page" featured the "Mafia Bible" which contained a plan to cause violence and mayhem in the school.

Apparently, advocating murder and mayhem via Internet is pretty common stuff. Alex Curtis operates a "White Racist" web site to distribute anti-Semitic and racist literature. Curtis allegedly urges others who share his beliefs to use such methods as biological weapons and selling poison-laced drugs as a well of killing.

Even more insidious is the case against Ryan Wilson, a neo-Nazi, who made death threats to fair housing advocate Bonnie Jouhari. Wilson admitted to the FBI that he had put images of Jouhari on his web site and labeled her a "race traitor.". He also said, "Traitors like this should beware, for in our day, they will be hung from around the neck from the nearest tree or lamp post."

Jouhari, who is white, worked at the ReadingBerks Human

Relations Council in Reading, Pennsylania as well as for the Hate Crimes Task Force in her county. Because she feared for her life and that of her daughter, Jouhari fled to Washington State.

In Jouhari's case, she had a staunch defender in then Housing and Urban Development Secretary Andrew Cuomo, now Governor of New York. He pursued and then welcomed a ruling by Chief Administrative Law Judge Alan Heifetz that Wilson, and his Philadelphia-based neo-Nazi group ALPHA HQ, had violated the Fair Housing Act by making death threats against a fair housing advocate on the Internet and in a television interview.

In the United States we are bounded by the First Amendment which guarantees free speech. However, the Internet is global and other countries are not so forgiving. A landmark ruling in France saw Yahoo! threatened with severe legal action for allowing the auctioning of Nazi memorabilia on its sites. The sales of such good are prohibited by French law. Although Yahoo waged a fierce legal battle against this ruling the company ultimately capitulated and banned this sort of auction across all of its sites as has eBay.

Meanwhile, attempts are being made to attack racist sites across the web. Don Black and his Stormfront site are engaged in litigation with the Dr Martens footwear empire, for hosting sites that "tarnish the image" of the boots popular with skinheads. More importantly, Jewish groups have threatened action against governments who are failing to deal with new laws to ban neo-Nazi materials.

Lest one thinks that the First Amendment should be repealed in light of this high-tech age, think again. A federal judge in Seattle reinforced the right of people online to speak their minds, even anonymously. The judge ruled that a company involved in litigation can't force disclosure of the identities of people who anonymously blasted the company on the Web. Judge Thomas Zilly wrote that the First Amendment clearly applies to the Internet even though the critics said downright nasty things about the company and its officers, calling them "cheating, thieving, stealing, low-life criminals".

Way back in the ancient days of the Internet (1997) a three day conference on hate and the Internet was organized by B'nai Brith Canada. Most speakers agreed that free speech is important. Nadine Strossen, president of the American Civil Liberties Union at the time, called it "the lifeblood of the democratic system". Strossen's view was that stifling even the most hateful speech is wrong for a variety of reasons. One reason is that stopping people from expressing these views does not stop people from holding these views. She reasons that hate propagandists are better combated by letting them say what they have to say and then responding to them rather than by trying to muzzle them.

The Anti-Defamation League wrote the definite treatise on the legal issues affecting Internet hate speech. In "Combating Extremism in Cyberspace" the ADL takes on the important question of whether hate speech should be regulated in a free speech democracy.

The Internet generation, unfortunately, is seriously at risk of infection by this virus of hate. Not only is this virus present on the Internet today; it is being spread around the globe, in the wink of an eye - or, more accurately, with the click of a mouse. This exciting new medium allows extremists easier access than they have ever had before to a potential audience of millions, a high percentage of whom are young and gullible. It also allows haters to find and communicate cheaply and easily with like-minded bigots across borders and oceans, to promote and recruit for their cause while preserving their anonymity, and even share instructions for those seeking to act out their intolerance online.

Most hate sites are expert on what you can and cannot say vis-a-vis the First Amendment. Some speech is indeed unprotected. For example, if the speech contains a direct, credible "true" threat against an identifiable individual, organization or institution.

While hate sites might be First-Amendment savvy, their followers seldom are. 21-year old Richard Machado sent a threatening e-mail signed "Asian Hater" to 60 Asian students at the University of California at Irvine. In this e-mail Machado stated that he hated Asians and that if Asians were not at UCI the school would be much more popular. Of course, none of what Machado said up until this point can be considered illegal. It was the next part of the message that got him into hot water,

I personally will make it my life career to find and kill every one of you personally. OK????? That's how determined I am ..... Asian Hater.

A jury convicted Mercado on two counts of federal civil rights violations. What's also interesting to note about this case is that Mercado is a naturalized American from Guatemala demonstrating the tribalism (i.e. minority vs. minority) discussed at the beginning of this chapter.

The flip-side of this incident (Latino vs. Asian) is the case of Kingman Quon, an Asian, who received a two year sentence for sending threatening e-mails to Latino professors, students and employees at the Massachusetts Institute of Technology and California State University at Los Angeles. The racially derogatory messages, which stated that Quon would "come down and kill" them, discussed his hatred of Latinos and accused them of being too "stupid" to get a job, or accepted as students, without the help of affirmative action.

The biggest win for those opposed to hate speech is the case of Planned Parenthood of Columbia/Willamette versus the American Coalition of Life Activists. The ACLA has an anti-abortion stance which is certainly permissible under the First Amendment. However, a Federal Jury determined that this loosely affiliated coalition of abortion groups were liable - to the tune of $100 million in damages - for making threats against abortion service providers.

The "Nuremberg Files" first appeared on the Internet in 1997. It listed the names of some 200 doctors who allegedly performed abortions along with detailed information about what they looked like, where they lived as well as the names of their spouses and children.

Headlined "Visualize Abortionists on Trial" and depicting blood dripping from aborted fetus parts, the site called for these persons to be brought to justice for crimes against humanity as the Nazis were after WWII. The names of these doctors who had been wounded were listed in gray. Doctors who had been killed by anti-abortionists had been crossed out.

The Internet is a global medium. As we've already seen, Yahoo and eBay have succumbed to pressure made by EU countries to ban the sale of Nazi memorabilia online. Companies that benefit from a global market can now be governed in all they do by any of the countries or regions in which they do business. The squelching of the GE-Honeywell merger by the European Union's Commissioner for Competition is testament to this new principle.   The EU adopted a four year 25-million Euro "action plan" on promoting safer use of the Internet by combating illegal and harmful content including racist and xenophobic ideas. So, though free speech laws predominate in the US, expect to see American sites that depend on global sales and good will back very far away from permitting free reign to hate.

The Internet is a series of hubs that are all interconnected. Most companies and individuals that create web sites do not "roll their own" so to speak. Instead they "rent out space" on someone else's computer. That someone else is referred to as an Internet Service Provider (ISPs). While the courts have ruled that ISPs are not themselves responsible for the content that they host for others, the ISP is certainly not ruled out of the economic food chain and can be cajoled into "doing the right thing."

Many free hosting ISPs have bans against "hate propaganda" and "hate mongering". This hate-free mindset is being quickly adopted by other ISPs. As was to be expected, this change in policy angered racists and bigots alike,

Next time some weak-minded individuals who can't stand the heat of the jew censor, you only take it as an opportunity to be stronger and freer to do what needs to be done. The Nationalist Observer will dump jew-corroded AOL .... I endorse all racialists to dump AOL as well and whenever the opportunity arises, to do as much physical or financial damage to AOL as possible.

ISPs are not immune from economic pressures which result when their subscribers or clients suggest that cancellation is imminent if the ISP continues to host offending sites. Economic boycott is an excellent methodology for dealing with recalcitrant ISPs. Clients of Cloudflare should be quite aghast that the company that hosts their websites are also host to the "white pride" purveying stormfront.org.

Universities are normally bastions of free speech, as they should be. However, sometimes tenured professors hold and disseminate views so repugnant to society that they should be censored. They often are but some universities hold fast to the notion that the freedom of speech wins no matter how uncivilized - and detrimental to society - the content of the message.

Northwestern University is home to Holocaust denier Arthur Butz. Although he is an Associate Professor of electrical and computer engineering at Northwestern University, which is a private college located in Illinois, Northwestern evidently sees nothing wrong in letting Butz use Northwestern's Internet servers to host Butz's web site discussing his revisionist views on the Holocaust.

Henry S. Bienen, president of Northwestern, insists that

Northwestern does not share Butz's revision views (i.e. "The Holocaust is not an issue for debate any more than the issue of whether the earth is round is a matter for debate"). In permitting Butz to maintain his non-professorial related web site on the Holocaust, Bienen claims that the NWU network is a free and open forum for the expression of ideas, including viewpoints that are strange, unorthodox, or unpopular.

I cannot see any moral, educational or economic justification for universities to permit unlimited free hosting of web sites for non-university and non-academic related purposes. The University of Illinois has just this policy. It supplies space only for web sites "in support of the educational, research and public service missions of the University."

Another way we can combat hate and extremism is through education. Certainly, diversity training has been playing an increasingly important role in recent years. Unfortunately, diversity training is often dull and consequently few really (stay awake long enough to) get the message.

One person that has the ability to keep folks awake is Scary Guy which is, believe it or not, his legal name. Scary, a one time buttoned-down, suited up sales guru for computer-maker Unisys Corp. always had a secret passion - tattoos. Under that blue suit, white shirt and black tie was a panorama of undulating, colorful images.

After Scary left Unisys he opened several tattoo parlors and uncovered all of his artwork. A competitor he didn't even know ran an ad in the newspaper that said, "are you tired of dealing with scary guys with war paint facial tattoos".

Well, I never met this individual and was wondering why anyone would say such a thing about someone they don't even know .... let alone put it in the paper. The first thought in my mind was revenge. What can I do to get back at him? I thought about suing him and I thought about running a negative ad. But my salesperson training taught me never to put your competition down. I decided to go the next step. I put myself up on a pedestal.

I told myself that I was just better than this guy. I don't do these things. And then one day I was sitting in the office of one of my tattoo parlors and the thought came to me that I was also a prejudiced person - just like the guy that ran the ad. I went home and told my wife that I was packing my bags to travel the world to help people see each other differently.

He's been traveling ever since. Scary has spoken to more than a million people and been on 75 talk shows all espousing the same tolerance message. He talks about prejudice as the result of fear and lack of knowledge.

How does the Internet fit into all of this? Although Scary realizes that, like film, the Internet is a vast repository of violent and hateful imagery, he also sees that it can be used to expose the root of hate,

I think that exposing hate is good. Haters become haters not because they are exposed to hate. It's because their emotional intelligence is not there. They just don't have the knowledge to deal with themselves.

In the end it will most likely be economics that changes the way the Internet "behaves". In fact, it just might change the way we all behave. Richard Butler, now deceased, was the founder of the neo-Nazi Aryan Nations. He used to teach a rather nasty message from his compound in Idaho. Then some of the men guarding his gate beat up and shot at a woman and her son. The jury found Butler responsible and awarded the family $6 million, forcing Butler to forfeit his land. Now Greg Carr owns the land and he intends to turn it into a center for civil rights education. Carr, born in Idaho and now living in Boston, is the millionaire founder of the Prodigy Internet service. There just might be some justice in the Internet world.

@GOD

Genesis, Chapter 1, Release 2.0
#In the beginning was the computer. And God said :Let there
be light!
#You have not signed on yet. :God.
#Enter user password. :Omniscient.
#Password Incorrect. Try again! :Omnipotent.
#Password Incorrect. Try again! :Technocrat.
#And God signed on at 12:01 a.m., Sunday, March 1 :Let there
be light!
#Unrecognizable command. Try again! :Create light.
#Done.
:Run heaven and earth.
#And God created Day and Night.

And then there was the Internet - give or take a few million years. The little ditty that opened this chapter may have first been published on alt.tasteless.jokes, the Internet's original repository for questionable humor, but more than a few people actually equate the mysteries of the Internet with the mysteries of God.

Jonathan Rosen is a novelist and essayist interested in understanding the dichotomy of the Talmud. The Talmud, for those not in the know, is a vast compilation of Judaic law. The core contents of the Talmud were edited by the end of the 5th century CE and contains elucidations, elaborations, commentaries and even debates between rabbis - sometimes separated by centuries.

I realized that what interests me is learning to embrace contradictory forces: ancient tradition and contemporary chaos, doubt and faith, the living and the dead, tragedy and hope.

When Rosen's grandmother died he took solace in the poetry of John Donne. But there was one phrase he couldn't quite remember so he took to the Internet to locate it.

For one moment, there in dimensionless, chilly cyberspace, I felt close to my grandmother, close to John Donne, and close to some stranger who, as it happens, designs software for a living.

As we all know the Internet is a place where we can "wander out of the wilderness for a while, ask a question and receive an answer." Here is where Rosen sees a real parallel to the Talmud - both are places where everything exists - if only you know how and where to look.

The Talmud helped Jews survive after the destruction of the Temple by making Jewish culture portable and personal. In the same way, there are elements in the inclusiveness of the Internet well suited to a world that is both more uprooted and more connected than ever before. Finding a home inside exile, finding a self inside infinity, finding a self inside a set of competing voices was an ancient challenge and is a modern one too.

More than 80% of Americans believe in a spiritual being. Of course, more than a few percentage points were probably contributed by people who responded in the affirmative just to be on the safe side. Nevertheless, Americans are still quite a religious lot.

Sherry Turkle in her seminal work "Life on the Screen" reports that numerous computer users she has interviewed talk of their online experience in spiritual terms. People, evidently with a straight face, tell her that computer networks resonate with our most profound sense that life is not predictable. Turkle cites one interviewee who concludes, "To me, it's God coming together with science, and computers have made it all possible".

In the late 1800's, a young impoverished French girl saw a series of apparitions that would lead her to Sainthood. Whether St. Bernadette of Lourdes actually saw and heard the Virgin Mary is, of course, open to speculation but there is absolutely no doubt that she believed she saw what she saw and heard what she heard. Hundreds - even thousands - of others have seen "miracles" over the millennia. From burning bushes to bleeding statutes. What all of these people have in common is great faith.

Since so many modern people also profess to having this same great spiritual faith it should come as no surprise that people see God virtually everywhere. Who does not feel spiritual when confronted by the grandeur of the Grand Canyon or the quiet and stillness of Arcadia?

This is the forest primeval. The murmuring pines and the hemlocks, bearded with moss, and in garments green, indistinct in the twilight, stand like Druids of eld, with voices sad and prophetic, Stand like harpers hoar, with beards that rest on their bosoms. Loud from its rocky caverns, the deep-voiced neighboring ocean speaks, and in accents disconsolate answers the wail of the forest.

Henry Wadsworth Longfellow wrote Evangeline in the mid 1800's. It recounts the expulsion of the French Arcadians out of their homelands of present-day Nova Scotia. While political in nature, the prose presents such a vivid description of the beauty of the place, that countless schoolchildren have memorized its passages. I was one of those children, and to this day I cannot hike or drive through a forest without repeating the passage I excerpted above. It's my homage to something that I find quite spiritual.

I cannot, however, find the same spirituality in the Internet. Nor can any of the dozen or so friends and acquaintances I queried on the topic. Turkle, on the other hand, insists that people really do see the Net as a new metaphor for God. Her reasoning is that they experience electronic networks, like life itself, evolving by a force they can neither understand, nor control. She explains that the Internet is one of the most dramatic examples of something that is self-organized, which is exactly the point. God is also a distributed, decentralized system.

We see what we want to see and many see the spiritual in all the most unlikely places. Neither I nor my friends are particularly religious and most of us have been weaned on the computer so, perhaps for us, the spirituality of the network is all but impossible to see. The vast majority of the world, however, is just coming up to speed on the computer and is, most certainly, more religious than I am. Perhaps these are the folks that Turkle interviewed.

The question is, in successive generations, as computers become more and more infused into our everyday activities - to a point where we don't recognize the point where the computer begins and we end - will those that Turkle interview still feel the same way?

Charles Henderson is the Executive Director of the Association for Religion and Intellectual Life. He contends that in this postindustrial society, traditional symbols and metaphors of the spiritual life have been deconstructed and rendered irrelevant to human experience. Science has driven a sharp wedge between people's sense of how this world really works and the traditional, religious view of how it is supposed to work. He insists that with the waning power of certain religious symbols, others rise to take their place. The Internet, according to Henderson, has indeed risen.

If the Internet is coming to be seen as a metaphor for God, it is not because the metaphor dropped magically from heaven, but by the same process through which most religious symbols have been born; naturally out of the everyday experience of real people. God spoke from the mountaintops to people living near the mountains; God was spoken of as King when real kings ruled the nations of the earth; likewise, in the information age, God will be perceived as being in and through that network which connects us with each other and with the world in which we live. In some ways that network is the Internet.

What Henderson is really saying is that we tend to view our presents and our futures while always looking backwards to our pasts. Marshall McLuhan said this even more succinctly,

When faced with a totally new situation, we tend always to attach ourselves to the objects, to the flavor of the past. We look at the present through a rear-view mirror. We march backwards into the future.

Then there are the irreverent folks. These guys want to eliminate God altogether and go right to the Internet.

You were born, and you can't remember anything before you existed. When you don't exist, you won't remember existing .... This hurts. So we at least want the illusion that somehow, an ethereal audience will be watching. God has to explain why things happen to us. Why did she leave me? Why did he die? Life is horribly unfair. God is ethereal.

Somehow God is smeared out all over the Universe and is able to watch all of us at the same time, able to judge us and what is in our hearts and evaluate our deeds ..... A little far-fetched if you ask me. So I have a humble suggestion. If we are going to fall back on our hierarchical primate biology and feel the need to create the illusion that someone is watching at least let us make it something real .... I Propose we forget God, and go with the Internet ..... There really are

people out there [on the Internet]. .. The Internet is people. Websites, newsgroups,
webcams   We've created these so we can be watched
Somehow we are less lonely this way ..... Somehow we have friends who actually respond when we ask them questions, not like God who never answers.

Spirituality - or lack of spirituality - aside, most theologians see a much more practical side of the Internet. They see it as a means to convey "the word."

Getting the word out

Religion has always played a very large role in our lives. Whenever a new technology arises "the word" is one of the first things to be automated. Many of the prehistoric cave paintings we've uncovered depict sometimes crude, sometimes masterful, renderings of undoubtedly religious or spiritual significance to our ancient brethren. The Renaissance, the zenith of human artistic expression, saw the creation of Michelangelo's Sistine Chapel. Johanes Gutenberg's printing press turned out the Bible as its first product.

Closer to our own time, the fledging motion picture industry produced several biblical films including the "Lear Passion" in 1897 and "The Horitz Passion Play" in the same year. In the early twenties Cecil B. DeMille produced the first biblical blockbuster, "The Ten Commandments" followed by "The King of Kings". Religion evidently sells.

Religion works on TV too. From Billy Graham to Oral Roberts to Jim and Tammy Bakker, religionists have taken to the airwaves like a duck takes to water.

So it's natural that this latest medium, the Internet, should attract much the same crowd - and then some. But just how is the Internet being used?

I will guess that the use falls into five broad categories. First, people find on-line religion a good reference tool for locating churches, church organizations and documents. Second, it serves a study or educational need: People can learn from its content. Third, some on-line religious material provides the high-tech equivalent of spiritual reading. It nourishes and lifts the spirit in a contemporary and interactive way. Fourth, on-line religion can foster a kind of community - at least a virtual community - with like-minded individuals. Indeed, a number of sites encourage a more conscious community through chat rooms and bulletin board discussions. And fifth, those Internet sites confirm and validate people who see their beliefs, churches, organizations, pastors, schools and so forth on-line.

There are 2.4 billion Christians worldwide. Of these, 87 million are Internet users. While Christians may be the predominant religion of users on the Internet, they are by no means the only religious - or anti-religious group to take advantage of "God in the ether".

In 1998 Nansook Hong published a book which describes in harrowing detail her 14 years of abuse at the hands of the Moon family, and her eventual escape. Her tale has it all - sex, tax evasion, money laundering, drugs, abuse and even incest.

You remember the esteemed Reverend Sun Myung Moon, don't you? Deceased in 2012, he was the Unification Church leader reputed to be a cult leader. In 1992 Debbie Diglio's son John went off to New York University. One weekend, shortly into his first semester, he went away for a weekend and simply vanished. His roommate told his mother that he had gone away with some new friends who were from a group known as CARP. Turns out that CARP, an acronym for Collegiate Association for the Research of Principles, was a front group for the Unification Church. Thus began a frantic search for John. The Unification Church, after all, had been accused by critics of brainwashing impressionable young people into becoming robotic followers of Moon as a new messiah.

I was a dedicated core member of CARP from 1986 to 93. I initially was invited to a cup of tea at an "international student club" by two Japanese students in San Francisco. A cup of tea that was to cost me 6 1 /2 years of my youth, my family and a mountain of emotional and financial resources. Through a well designed array of deceptive recruiting and manipulative indoctrination techniques, I was systematically stripped of my critical thinking abilities and transformed from a liberal agnostic to an extremist right wing religious fanatic .... within a matter of weeks. I was made to stay illegally in the US, to illegally sell pictures and flowers to raise money - even at subzero temperatures, living with 11 people in a Ford van without pay, social or medical insurance. I worked 18 to 20 hours on average, 7 days a week, 360 days a year, not allowed to see my family and friends ... My leader even forbid me to attend a church service with the argument "you're not a Christian.".

Although he's dead, he lives on through the Internet. The Family Federation for a Heavenly USA is like a siren call to a new generation of weak-willed, addle-brained young people.

Perhaps the most interesting of Internet-related cults came to a tragic end when its members committed mass suicide in late March 1997. Heaven's Gate was typical of cults in that it was headed by a charismatic leader by the name of Bo Applewhite. They embraced a secularist version of the Christian Rapture, believing that a star trailing the Halle Bopp comet was actually a spaceship ready to transport them, once they had rid themselves of their bodies or "earthy containers."

What's interesting about Haven's Gate is that its followers were no bunch of dummies. Not only did they have their own web site, they also developed web sites for a living. Unlike the Moonies whose followers sold sickly flowers, the Heaven's Gate cultists sold slick web sites. The Internet offers unparalleled opportunities for seeking new converts and to espouse a message. The sci-fi pastiche of Heaven's Gate was a most perfect fit.

According to Wendy Gale Robinson of the Department of Religion at Duke University, cult member Yvonne McCurdy-Hill left five children and all her worldly possessions to join the group after finding it on the Web. She says,

Freedom from the physical body and the free reign given to the imagination in cyberspace .... could have contributed to the cult members' decision to go the next, if illogical step ... .It's within the realm of possibility that Applewhite's ministry plus cyberculture was a toxic mix.

The Internet is quite an economical medium for cults. E-mail and web pages are cheap and both keep cult members hooked, whatever their location, with messages of support, love - and ultimately propaganda. Those cults entirely Internet based don't even have to rent land or buildings. The Internet becomes their virtual commune.

Professor Margaret Singer, an emeritus professor of psychology at the University of California at Berkeley says that cult joiners have little or no street smarts.

College-age and young working types spend hours in front of their computers and the only friendships they have are other people on the computer. And they're open to being too trusting and thinking what they read is true.

And what they read is often a glowing, if fictitious, account of what it's like to be a member of that particular group. Feeling lonely, alienated or just plain upset by one or more seemingly insurmountable problems, quite a few people are ripe for the pickin.

Should we be worried about this? Most certainly. Should we take some action to prohibit these fringe groups from using the Internet? Here's what Bruce Lawrence, Professor Emeritus in the Department of Religion at Duke University, has to say,

Yes, kooks are out there, along with genuine, honest geeks, but I think that the benefits of digital dharma far outweigh the downsides.

The Internet provides an almost unlimited resource for researching the tenets of any religion - past, present and maybe even future - that we might be interested in. From Scientology (16 million hits according to Google) to Satanism (211 million hits), there are news groups and web sites to fit any religious palate.

Asatru (3 million hits) is, according to www.asatru.org, the ethnic religion of the indigenous Northern European People. "It is the religion of our ancestors, one of the oldest still in practice, dating back to the beginning of this branch of the human race, some 40,000 years ago". According to the Alexa Traffic, this site ranks 2,355,058. Compare this to the New York Times, which ranks 104.

When Martin Luther posted his 95 theses on the door of a church it was as if they almost magically appeared. It was magic alright - the magic of the printing press. In the same way, the "magic of the Internet" throws the doors open to anyone with a cause and a web site. Like Martin Luther, some of these "religions" are considered heresies by the older, established religious order - but the Internet enables them to persevere - if somewhat in obscurity.

On the Internet we find the First Cyberchurch of the Scientific God; the First Internet Church of All; and even ecospirituality - an attempt to give the environmentalist ethic a spiritual dimension by invoking Gaia which is Earth as a living, divine being. We even find something called technosophy, whose tagline appears to be "Deus ex machina," which aims to promote a spiritual appreciation for technology. By the way, one of technosophy's precepts is to define our own bodies as sophisticated collections of technological systems. We are indeed the machine.

While the fringe is adequately, if humorously, represented online, the Internet is also home to the more mainstream religions as well as that which lies between mainstream and fringe.

Christians have been trying to convert non-Christians for years (make that millennia) - particularly Jews. None have been more zealous than Jews for Jesus. Moishe Rosen, now deceased, was the founder of this particular group. Everything Rosen did he did online. "For the past four years I have been ministering in Chat Rooms and posting my messages on bulletin boards."

When Jewish People are wondering if Jesus just might be the promised Messiah they are not likely to drop by a church or attend a discussion. Just their wondering would be seen as a betrayal to our fellow Jews, so anonymity is important. In the past they might inquire in a library or bookstore. Many might stand for a while and listen to a street preacher expositing the scriptures. Now the Internet is the crossroad and marketplace of ideas. Because they can be anonymous, many Jews are coming online to investigate the claims of Christ.

Anonymity is one of the major benefits of the Internet. For religionists, it is a double-edged sword. As Rosen suggests, it enables those that seek information and/or conversion to do so in the privacy of their own homes - without exacting the wrath of family or friends. On the other hand, it does open doors that mainstream religionists might prefer to keep shut.

Sulayman X converted to Islam in 1993 and lives in a large Asian city. He also runs a web site called Queer Jihad. But while his web site gives him the freedom of expression, that same freedom of expression sends a barrage of hate mail his way.

The most neutral of religious web sites isn't really a religion site at all. Instead, beliefnet.com is a clearing house where everyone, no matter what his or her religion, can come together to share prayers, debate and just discuss all things spiritual. Beliefnet features prayer circles in which a Jew may post a question to a Wiccan. Users may leave wedding notices, participate in meditations, create memorials and read a wide variety of articles - everything from fasting to sex.

The Jewish community has its websites too. One of the first was Jewish.co.uk. One of its best features was "Ask the rabbi." So I did. In response to my question on the value of the Internet in religion, Rabbi Leslie Solomon said,

Judaism bases itself on an intellectual foundation. Jews have always been literate and well-versed in the Jewish ways to live. The modern era has seen the emancipation of Jews from their traditional books into the modern universities. Jews have excelled in most areas of intellectual concern, be it medicine, law, science, etc. As the traditional societal structure has broken down in many parts of the world in terms of Jewish secondary and tertiary schooling, new modes of education have arisen. The boom in English language Jewish books and especially the Internet has allowed remote Jews to become re-educated and re-affiliated to their roots. The spiritual and emotional attachments to religion remain unaddressed by the Internet.

Unfortunately, this website is no more. However, you can still ask a question. Just do a Google search for "ask a rabbi."

Stephanie Krill DiMaulo always dreamed of a traditional wedding ceremony under a gazebo surrounded by blossoms, blessed by a Roman Catholic priest. Unfortunately, the church does not approve of weddings outside of church buildings. So she had to look elsewhere. That elsewhere was the Internet - sometimes called "God's Yellow Pages Online", Stephanie found Father George and her blossom strewn wedding went off without a hitch.

It has been suggested that over 35 percent of the U.S.

population is using the Internet for religious purposes. In addition, other numbers reveal that one out of six teens say that within the next five years they expect to use the Internet as a substitute for current church-based religious experience. One site that does this today is chatnow.org.

For the most part, online churches are started by those that seek to balance the bad of the Internet with the god as was the case with the Reverend Dr. Everett A. Brown,

St. John's began in January, 1998, and went online in March, 1998, as an independent online Church. I had seen so many bad things on the Internet that I felt something good -- something that spreads the Gospel of our Lord and Savior Jesus Christ needed to be online. At that time I could not find a Church service online -- only some Church ads or webpages that gave information about specific Churches. I was hoping for maybe a thousand log-ons by the end of 1998. To my surprise we had over 25,000. Currently we average around 23,000 log-ons each quarter. St. John's tries to be as traditional as possible even though it operates entirely online. One advantage it has is that the service is available 24 hours a day, seven days a week. The sermon is changed each week. Another advantage it has is that many people can discuss situations or problems that are of concern and ask for prayer to help deal with those concerns without being embarrassed.

For the most part, religious web sites are poorly designed amalgams of gospel, chat, bulletin boards and a bit of e-commerce. One religious web site that has all of these features and is also well designed is one run by the brothers of Christ in the Desert.

At the end of a red-clay road in northwestern New Mexico is the Monastery of Christ. Inside the warm brown adobe building can be heard the hum and buzz of computers. Using electricity generated by a dozen solar panels the brothers tend to their home page and to their business of designing and maintaining other people's web sites.

Brother Mary-Aquinas, who was once a systems analyst in Denver, is one of those monks,

I can't think of better work for us to be doing. This work goes back to the ancient tradition of the scribes, taking information and making it beautiful, into art. In a certain sense, the Web and what will happen in the next decade is a return to that tradition ..... For years it was small -- three to four monks -- and we could get by in revenues from our guest house and our gift shop. Then we got on the Internet -- it seemed a good opportunity to supplement our library so the monks could do scholarly work -- and we found out about the Web. It seemed a good way to supplement our income since it is difficult to find creative work that adapts to the monastic schedule.

Religious institutions that don't establish a presence in cyberspace will start to seem badly out of touch. The failure to do so sends an important signal about the ability to advise people in an era of technological growth.

While single-focused religious web sites will continue to predominate (i.e. Jews will flock to Jewish web sites and Christians will flock to Christian web sites), the greatest hope for humanity actually lies in sites such as beliefnet.com. For it is only here where we can all mix it up. Buddhists can argue with Protestants, and Moonies can shoot the breeze with Mormons.

Posted to beliefnet.com Multi-Faith Forum. What Religion is God?

Posted 6128101 7:40 PM
People spend a lot of time here on Earth arguing and discussing which religion is the true religion. My question, what is God's religion Is he a Muslim. A Christian, a Hindu, or what? All religion is inspired by the reality of the spiritual and natural realms, and since God is the Creator of the spiritual and natural realms, all religions are in some way inspired by God. Is God above religion? Is religion something we humans put too much stock in? Should we just stop worrying about it? I don't know. Any ideas?

Posted 6128101 8:03 PM
The answer to the question is Christian, more specifically, Catholic.

Posted 6128101 9:08 PM
God doesn't need religion, humans do in the mistaken belief god needs it.

Posted 61291011:57 PM
I don't think God has any one religion, I think that all religions are paths to God, who is too big to be contained in anyone faith tradition or path.

Alvin Plantinga, a philosophy professor at Notre Dam, says that despite all of these disagreements, these electronic conversations will ultimately help people from many religions understand the common ideas that bind them together.

One of the sustaining causes of religious disagreement has been the sense of strangeness, of pure unfamiliarity. The communications revolution will not wash out the important differences, but we will learn to grade our differences in order of importance.

As Rached Ghannouchi, an Arab philosopher says,

The inhabitants of the small, networked world we have become have to find a way to understand each other. Otherwise, we are all doomed to annihilation.

#ATTENTION ALL USERS: COMPUTER GOING DOWN FOR REGULAR DAY OF MAINTENANCE AND REST IN FIVE MINUTES. PLEASE SIGN OFF.
:Create new world.
#You have exceeded your allotted file space. You must destroy old files before new ones can be created.
:Destroy earth.
#Destroy earth. Please confirm.
:Destroy earth confirmed.
#COMPUTER DOWN

@POLITICS

In a democracy, the highest office is the office of citizen. --- Supreme Court Justice Felix Frankfurther

The first thing I did when I started writing this book was send an e-mail to each and every Senator in our fair country. My mission was to find out which, if any, of these paid servants of the people would respond to my question about the future of social security. The answer, as I expected, was zilch. Nada. No one. Not even the Senators from my very own state gave me the time of day.

I did receive a bunch of auto-replies however which, more or less, told me that I would never get a reply " *.... we get an overwhelming number of e-mail messages. Unfortunately .....* So much for cyberdemocracy.

Actually, in spite of recalcitrant U.S. Senators (and Representatives), there is an overwhelming case to be made for government, and all its attendant functions, to go online. As you will see in this chapter this is happening now. However, when you couple the advances of technology with the fact that today's wired youth are tomorrow's cyber-citizens then cyberdemocracy should be all but assured in, at least, the most democratic and wealthy of countries.

There will be bumps along the way, unfortunately.

Cyberdemocracy is not solely the process of bringing government online. For cyberdemocracy to work, there must also be an avenue for a government's citizens to voice their opinions as well as for the media to analyze the issues and present its conclusions. So cyberdemocracy (sometimes referred to as E-mocracy) is a three headed beast - government, advocacy and media.

During the boom period of the late 90's there was a plethora of politically-oriented web sites out there. The millennium bust crushed as many political start-ups as it did e-commerce startups. One, grassroots.com, even morphed into a website touting services for the public affairs arm of Edelman PR.

OneDemocracy.com was also one of the causalities. It's goal was laudable. As Jeff Karan, a co-founder of OneDemocracy.com put it,

With no more than a computer and a connection, members of OneDemocracy will be able to build their own networks of like-minded individuals around issues of personal importance and take collective action ..... OneDemocracy will be available for anyone from a grandmother trying to get a pothole fixed in her street, to a national organization lobbying to fix a hole in the Ozone layer.

Greg Gretsch was the second of OneDemocracy.com's co-founders. He was quoted as saying,

The Internet is radically changing the balance of power in American politics, just as television did decades ago. However, this time citizens will not just be passive recipients of information, they will have the tools to become active participants in the process.

Another casualty of the dot-com bust was PoliCast.com. PoliCast was run by Gary Barrett, a grizzled veteran reporter with over 26 years of experience dishing the political dirt at old-fashioned radio stations. Signing on as the first Internet-only radio station to specialize in political news and commentary,

Policast rose like a phoenix during the 2000 national political conventions, but just as quickly crashed back to earth when it ran out of money.

Most of the ones that went bankrupt did so because they tried to be too much too soon. Voter.com and Politics.com are two examples of sites that had a lot of venture capital, hired expensive editors, columnists and spent a lot of money for advertising. Problem was that their content differed little from other mainstream sites. Political sites that are thriving are the ones that offer levels of expertise or political slant that attract repeat readers. Newsmax.com is one example of a site that used word-of-mouth and a few big names to build their reputation as a source of political news for conservatives. They are using their mailing list to raise money by mass-marketing political merchandise and for the solicitation of political contributions. Politics.com tried to merge with another company-it fell through-then the holders of the majority stock tried to sell it for a million dollars and no one was interested.

The Internet is radically changing the balance of power in American politics, just as television did decades ago. But there are some major differences. The first is that, even with streaming sites such as NetFlix, there are a limited number of television channels to watch, which essentially means that each channel is guaranteed a rather nice fat percentage of viewers. During the ascendancy of television as a political device during the 1960 campaign, there were only three major channels. Even with the advent of cable and satellite the number of stations is still well below 500. Compare this to the millions and millions of web sites available for viewing. In addition, television comes accompanied by various directories and guides helping people quickly find their way to the show of their choice. TV Guide, listings in all the newspapers, and various cable guides all provide the couch potato with everything he or she needs to locate the very next installment of Survivor. The Internet, although the beneficiary of a wide variety of search engines, lacks anything even remotely comparable to the thoroughness and descriptiveness of TV Guide. Finding anything on the Internet is a real challenge. Getting noticed by all those millions of web surfers when there are millions of "channels" to choose from is even more of a challenge.

Traditional television production revolves around the concept of broadcasting - the key word here is "broad." This means that broadcasters try to reach as many people (i.e. as broad an audience) as possible. Political coverage on television is usually limited to the news, talk shows (occasionally interactive via phone, e-mail and web site) and convention/election coverage. It's a well known fact that most news organizations have heavy costs and that these costs are subsidized by sitcoms, game shows and other light fare that substitutes for entertainment nowadays. Whatever my criticisms on the quality of today's television line-up, I applaud television's decision to continue its long tradition of news coverage. Internet sites do not have a similar cost-allocation formula.

The Internet operates on the principle of narrowcasting. There are millions of web sites out there in the ether. While some, like MSNBC and eBay, are most definitely focused towards broad audiences, most web sites are focused on particular constituencies such as voters in Indiana or people interested in 17th century English poetry. Narrowly focused news sites, advocacy sites and political sites need to be funded directly either through memberships, donations or fees collected via advertising. Given the share volume of these sites there simply isn't enough revenue to go around.

Richard Davis, a professor of political science at Brigham Young, wrote *The Web of Politics: The Internet's Impact on the American Political System* (Oxford University Press, 1998). Davis's oft-stated thesis is that,

The Internet will not lead to the social and political revolution so widely predicted. Because they are effectively adapting to the Internet, the existing power structure, traditional media, and powerful groups will continue to dominate the production of political news and information, the expression of opinion, and the mobilization of political participation. Internet users will continue to be the affluent, the already politically interested and active. Because there is not an adequate tool for political involvement by the public, there will be no rise of Internet democracy in which people become political activists through acquiring information.

Davis has touched on several interesting issues in his polemic against the value of cyberdemocracy. He makes a case for the Internet population being affluent and unchangeable. Actually, this is far from the truth. When I first started surfing the Web in the early 1990s, as a woman I was very much in a minority. At the time, the media decried "the gender gap." Today, more women than men are online. Unfortunately, it turns out that they are verbally attacked far more often than men proving, sadly, that misogyny lives online as well as off.

Davis then trots out the tired (I should say retired) statistic that the web is being surfed solely by the affluent. While the poor might not have access to their own PCs nor have an inclination to go to the library, their children certainly do make use of the Internet. The price of PCs has fallen dramatically and free Internet access (at least for a year) is often a come-on lure to get you to buy a PC making the Internet an attractive, and inexpensive purchase. With the advent of Internet accessibility on a smartphone and spectacular growth of social media venues like Facebook, Twitter, Snapchat, Instagram and TikTok, everyone has a megaphone to voice their political opinions.

So, the Internet is a ripe breeding ground for the middle-class, if not poor, disenchanted.

I came of age during the Vietnam war. I can't recall the

number of anti-war rallies I attended or committees I joined to end this or promote that. The sixties generation were definitely joiners.

The Big Chill was a great movie (with great stars) which brought together a group of old friends for a funeral. These old friends had been at college together during the sixties. Each was an activist that thought that his or her actions would most certainly change the world for the better. Decades later, when they met again for the funeral, they decried the fact that they had "sold out." They opted for the bucks over the advocacy. One had become a television star, another a high-priced attorney, still another owned a series of shoe stores. The Big Chill was fact, not fiction. It's sad to say but the advocacy of the sixties has been replaced by the complacency of middle age - and the younger generations have not picked up the ball and run with it in any large way – until rather recently.

When George W. and his Supreme Court henchmen stole the 2000 election one would have expected riots in the street or at least millions of people gathering in front of the White House in protest. Of course, there were some protests but these were small in scale and mostly overlooked by the media. In spite of what some considered to be a coup d'etat most of us just went back to our TV s to watch the Super Bowl. Sadly, the same can be said for the 2016 election – which was stolen by Russian interference, gerrymandering, and James Comey's unforgiveable actions.

A few of us will always plod on - no matter what the odds. Because the Internet provides us with the ability to receive an unimpeded information flow (i.e. not censored by the government, in spite of Donald Trump's efforts), it is indeed possible to find like-minded folk and "get involved."

Consider MoveOn.org. This was an online effort to defeat congressional representatives who voted to impeach President Clinton. Today MoveOn is busy providing a forum for citizens "to counter the influence of monied interests and partisan extremes." But is it effective? Joan Blades, of Move On, answers this question,

... The Internet allowed us to be remarkably active online, on the phone and in person. Better still it enables and encourages new groups of citizens to participate - single parents with limited time, disabled people and younger folks that are Internet savvy. Is it as effective as taking to the streets? I guess that depends upon what you take to the streets and who you meet there.

Even the World Trade and G8 demonstrators got together online first before they traveled to Seattle and Genoa. Paradoxically, if you're serious about opposing capitalism and globalization you need e-mail, one of the fruits of both capitalism, to do it.

Of course, this last group has proven themselves to be rather extreme. Referring to themselves as anarchists they didn't further their cause by rioting. It is this extremism that troubles so many experts. Cass Sunstein, a professor of law at the University of Chicago is one of these experts. Sunstein and various social scientists have described a phenomena, which they refer to as "group polarization", in which like-minded people in an isolated group reinforce each others views, which then harden into extreme positions (think Timothy McVeigh and like-minded white supremacists).

Sunstein considers polarization to be just one of the negative political effects of the Internet. In his view, it permits people to filter out unwanted information, tailor their own news and congregate at special web sites that carefully reflect their own views. In other words, if you are a died-in-the wool anarchist who hates capitalism you are not likely to go to sites that support capitalism. Instead, you are probably going to subscribe to Facebook groups and visit web sites of like-minded people. Few of these web sites or groups offer opposing views. Remarkably, this is the same charge leveled at many of the sites

I described in the chapter on @hate. No White Pride web site permits opposing views, nor do any Blackpride web sites.

Many political web sites rely on a combination of voting yay or nay on issues and the posting of associated comments on those issues as can be seen in this heart-felt comment about globalization on the quorum.org bulletin board,

English common law, on which our judicial system is founded, has become "globalized" and no longer recognizes the right to self-defense. No point in defending yourself again a rapist or man with a gun in Britain: you'll go to jail for life.

Globalization is simply a matter of allowing a bunch of two-bit ex-kingdoms, dictatorships, theocracies and "emerging" post-colonial nations to impose their history of serfdom on the rest of the world.

Global trade is a good thing, as far as it goes, but when we get involved in foreign entanglements beyond the exchange of goods and attempt to impose our standards on anyone else or allow anyone else to affect our domestic policy we consign ourselves to the trash heap of history

James Fishkin, a political scientist at the University of Texas, has said that such efforts at web democracy follow the model of debate in ancient Sparta called the Shout. The idea behind the Shout is that the candidate that got the loudest applause or shout would win. Fishkin warns,

Unless we make special efforts to implement more ambitious democratic possibilities, the Internet, left to its own devices, is going to give us an impoverished form of democracy in the form of the Shout.

None other than ex-President Clinton's old spinmeister Dick Morris is behind vote.com, a site which claims that more than 32 million votes have already been cast. Morris' take is that direct democracy is destined to replace representative democracy. Congress, Morris thinks, will become superfluous as it is forced to blow to tidal waves of online public opinion. Wouldn't this have been nice during the 2016 election? Hillary Clinton would have won.

But are there - and will there ever be - tidal waves of opinion? If half of all Americans didn't vote in the last election, do we really expect those missing in action to participate online? More importantly, is anyone out there really listening?

Vote.com's 32 million votes on a variety of topics from patient bill of rights to cloning were sent directly to Congress and the President via e-mail. The impact?

While we cannot attest to any specific impact, an increasing number of elected officials are beginning to pay more attention to those constituents who choose to make their voices heard through e-mail. This is an ongoing process but the impact from emails is growing.

The sad truth is that, at least for now, and in spite of the best intentions of these web sites, these votes and these opinions are largely ignored. Congress and the President aren't able to ignore in-your-face protestors.

One of the best "in your face" tactics I have ever heard about was pioneered by lobbyist Jay Angoff. He wanted to vividly identify which Members of Congress who opposed mandatory warranty disclosures for used cars had received money from the used-car industry. He got a permit to set up a mock used-car lot in front of the Capitol, complete with junk cars. In order to get to the House floor, embarrassed legislators were forced to walk past the demonstrators and a gauntlet of TV news cameras.

The web, however, is a silent beast. It can't roar the way protestors can. And it's not as photogenic. What the web can do is provide the numbers. Those 32,000,000 vote.com votes did count for something. Of course, this number is the number of votes which coincides with a number of issues over a certain period of time. It's not 32 million separate individuals. I wish it were.

Just how many cyberactivists are out there? Forget the cyber. How many activists are out there? If you look at the statistics based on voting (i.e. Voting generally means you care about "the issues"), if you don't vote then you probably don't agitate. Over the past few decades the percentage of voters has dropped precipitously. About 50% of us vote during any given election. This means, obviously, that 50% of us don't vote - or don't give a damn. An estimated 24 million young people voted in 2016. That's great, but we need to do even better – particularly in 2020.

Since the future of activism depends on younger people getting into the groove - so to speak - it's really bad news that so many of them don't vote. Since they were reared on the 'Net and spend more time online then any other age category, I can deduce that if they don't get their news on-line they probably don't read newspapers offline either.

Activists don't grow on trees. They need to be nurtured. Perhaps the greatest activist - and nurturer - of all time is Ralph Nader, who has consistently issued a provocative challenge,

How many of you want to become leaders in the achievement of greater justice on earth? If not, why not? Could it be that the nation is suffering from an excess of leadership? Or is it more likely that our times reflect a massive escape from leadership responsibilities? With so much human activity conducted within and between larger and larger private and public bureaucracies, is it any wonder that the 'I only work here' syndrome has become an epidemic?

Can you imagine what would happen if people would turn off the TV and spend just ten hours a week exercising their citizenship .... There can be no daily democracy without daily citizenship. If we do not exercise our civic rights, who will? If we do not perform our civic

duties, who can? The fiber of a just society in pursuit of happiness is a thinking, active citizenry. That means you.

By demonstrating that an individual armed with facts, fortitude and creative zeal can actually achieve important reforms, Nader insists on the possibilities of democratic citizenship in a society dominated by institutional giants.

Doug Pinkham, President of Public Affairs Council and Foundation for Public Affairs agrees wholeheartedly with Nader. He sees the Internet as a vast meeting ground where things can actually get done and the "powers that be" are just about ready to start listening,

People really are listening to what is being said on the Internet. There are many examples of this. Several years ago the FDIC tried to tighten up its reporting rules for banks in an effort to curb money laundering. After receiving several hundred thousand e-mails from the Libertarians (who were concerned about privacy violations), however, they backed down from their proposed rulemaking. The major telecommunications legislation that passed several years ago featured major grassroots campaigns from both sides of the issue. Virtually every current public policy issue -- from the patients bill-of-rights to stem-cell research -- is being debated on the Internet and involves the use of grassroots technologies.

Recently, more and more activists are launching campaigns that "skip the middleman" and go directly to corporate CEOs, their Boards of Directors and major shareholders. Instead of lobbying Congress to pass laws that restrict corporate activities, they are applying pressure in other ways. The Rainforest Action Network is one of the major proponents of this approach. And it does have an impact.

I don't see us moving toward direct democracy via the Internet. A lot has been written about this subject, but we're still a long way off. Do you, as an average citizen, really want to get involved in budget deliberations for medical research? Do you want to vote

on the Internet when most people are still worried about sharing credit card information on the Net? To be sure, the Net will make our elected leaders more accountable and they will have access to much more information before casting their votes, but I think we'll stick with our representative democracy. The Founding Fathers knew what they were doing when they set up this form of government in the first place.

Nader's inspiration comes from Thomas Jefferson, who had written, "I know of no safer depository of the ultimate powers of society but the people themselves." But Jefferson could not have envisioned how monied special interests, official secrecy, procedural complexities , the brute size of the nation, and the corruption of some public officials would erode the sinews of government accountability.

Unless you've been hiding under a rock this past decade you can't help but notice how wrong everything seems. First, a person that most of us didn't vote for is squatting in the White House. Next, the Supreme Court turns out to be as partisan as any common thug -- I mean -- politician. Finally, we've got arsenic in our water, lead in our pipes, and oil leaks in the Artie tundra, and politicians who turn policy tricks for cash. And, oh yes, we've got climate change.

Actually things are better than they've ever been. That's because we've got the vote and the clout - if only we would use it. Not too long ago we didn't have clout - nor did many of us have the vote. According to Alex Keyssar, a professor of history and social policy at Harvard's Kennedy School, there have always been strong antidemocratic forces in the United States,

Large numbers of Americans throughout our history have not believed in universal suffrage and have acted accordingly. Their presence delayed the achievement of a fully enfranchised population until roughly 1970 and produced many episodes in which the right to vote contracted.

African-Americans were deprived of their right to vote for more than 70 years; women's suffrage was not adopted until 1920; Rhode Island imposed a property qualification on all foreign-born citizens for much of the 19th century; California went to great lengths to prevent Asians from voting. Even New York adopted an English language literacy test in 1921 that was active well into the 1960s.

Keyssar suggests that the decline in turnout in American elections, which began at the end of the 19th century, was not an accident. Turnout, he says, was reduced by laws designed to keep citizens from the polls and to prevent popular dissident parties from effectively contesting elections. He further suggests that both political parties have been key actors in this long running drama with neither having an unblemished record of embracing democratic principles,

This should not surprise us. The two major parties are in the business of winning elections rather than promoting democracy, and elections can be won by disenfranchising opponents, making it procedurally difficult for them to vote or not counting their votes at all.

Politicians have long tried to control voters. In cyberspace they're now trying to control what we say. Emerson, New Jersey should count itself lucky to have Stephen Moldow as a resident. In a show of citizenship that would make even Ralph Nader proud, Moldow donated his own time and money to set up a web page for the town. The web site is benign enough when you first look at it. It's got municipal information and minutes of township meetings. But if you look under the covers you'll find a controversy that got Moldow embroiled in a lawsuit.

Moldow was sued by two council members, a candidate for office and someone's husband because the web site also hosts a political message board where anything goes. It was to this forum that anonymous critics posted messages about elected officials -- accusing one of urinating in the pool and another of infidelity in marriage. This lawsuit, dismissed by the courts, was only one of a growing number of lawsuits across the country, which is quite worrisome to civil libertarians. Politicians, it would seem, are very thinskinned.

In spite of, or perhaps oblivious to, the inherent dangers of possibly losing our First Amendment rights to say anything we want, folks are still gathering at message boards like so many employees buzzing around a water cooler. And the stuff they're saying is often worth listening to. Just listen to a bit of a thread on one state = one vote on the speakout.com message boards.

If the Electoral College is abolished and only the Popular vote is used. Think about it. Everyone in the other 48 states. Would you want New York and California electing your President. Pleeeease .... I don't like the primaries as it is. To have a bunch of people that can barely start farm tractors establishing the Presidential front runner is crap.

And in response ....

I don't see what an ability to run farm machinery has to do with politics .... To suggest that all residents of a state should be lumped together into one vote, merely because of the way border lines are drawn is ludicrous. A far better policy would be to let each individual cast his or her vote the way he or she see fit, count those votes and declare the candidate who received the most votes the winner.

Gun control advocate Donna Dees-Thomases organized her Million Mom March to take advantage of the Internet. When she announced the march she also announced her Web site. It was here that visitors could register for the march, get information on how to get to Washington, and download handbooks on organizing and public relations.

Fifty state Web pages were created to help people who were working for the event better coordinate their local and national efforts. The web site was also used to raise funds by selling T-shirts and posters and even had the capability of accepting donations.

One of the best documented examples of using the Internet for advocacy was the International Campaign to Ban Land Mines. This group used the Internet to organize 1,400 activist groups in 90 countries in support of an international treaty. Campaign monitors filed daily email reports about activities around the world and armed with this information at least one group, the one from Australia, was able to pressure their delegation to vote against a proposed loophole in the treaty.

I didn't get a response from any of the Senators I sent my social security e-mail too. I bet, however, that if I said I wanted to donate money to their reelection campaign I'd get a speedy reply.

Our politicians may not be interested in using the Internet to foster a more direct approach to democracy but you can bet your booties that they've figured out how to use it to raise money..

With the help of some smart software these politicos have turned campaigning on its ear. This software matches voter files with other databases such as motor vehicle registrations and phone book entries. With the advent of social media, the software got even smarter. You can now target people right down to the color of their socks. President Obama perfected this technique in 2008 and 2012. Trump upped the ante in 2016, while the Russians wreaked havoc.

One site that the politicos would rather you not know about is opensecrets.org. Self-dubbed the "guide to the money in American elections" it has provided more than one case of heartburn by detailing just who's giving and who's receiving on Capitol Hill.

The government agency with the most ties to money, the dreaded IRS, was one of the first agencies to go online. From downloadable tax forms to filing online, the IRS has proven itself on the forefront of this latest incantation of the information revolution. More than a few governmental agencies are likeminded.

One of the courses I teach was "Web Concepts and Applications." During the first week I have my students write a short paper describing how their companies use the Internet. One of my students works for a remote California town in its Housing Authority which uses the Internet to pass information back and forth between the Housing Authority and HUD. Provoked by taking a class on web sites this student had this to say about what she'd like to do given the funding,

I think we should have a site that is versatile. One where anyone could go and apply for our services on-line and get the basics of programs we offer. I would also like to add a feature where tenants we currently house could read updated information about their complex such as activities going on, spray dates, etc., as well as be able to leave feedback. It would be a great service, in my opinion, to those that reply on others for transportation to be able to apply online and get answers.

A national survey conducted by Momentum Research Group Cunningham Communications, Inc. provides some insight into what services people really do want to be able to get online from their governments. Almost half of those surveyed said that they would like to use the Internet to renew their drivers' licenses. 38% said they wanted to use it to vote in major elections and 43% said they wanted to go online to renew their professional licenses. Most of these services are actually available today.

Today, it's hard to find a country or municipality without web access to information and services. Some leaders, however, probably wish the Internet had never been invented. Bangaryu Laxman, the former president of the main party in India's ruling coalition as well as India's former defense minister had to resign when the Internet opened up a nasty can of worms for them. It seems that Mr. Laxman accepted some money that looked very much like a bribe. The Internet press found out and it was curtains for Mr. Laxman.

Rutgers University's study, "The State of Electronically Enhanced Democracy" found that the Internet has enormous potential to strengthen democratic processes. The study found that many political web sites do not yet deliver on the promise of interactivity. Many of them simply post essays or catalog information. The researchers also described most of the political chat areas they encountered as "dead public space" where participants post comments but never receive replies.

One country where none of this matters is the tiny "country" of Sealand. During World War II the U.K. established a number of military bases in the form of sea forts along the east coast of England on the edge of the English territorial waters. One of these, located approximately 7 nautical miles from the coat, was situated in the international waters of the North Sea.

In 1967 one former English major, Paddy Roy Bates, formally occupied the island and settled there with his family. He proclaimed the island his own state and made himself Prince. By 1968 the British Navy sought to re-take the fort. Prince Roy of Sealand actually fired warning shots across the bows of these British destroyers.

Taken to court and accused of extensive crimes, Prince Roy actually won this one. The courts declared it is was not competent to exert any jurisdiction outside of British national territory. In saying this the court issued a de factor recognition of the Principality of Sealand. In 1999 Prince Roy, in ill health, deeded control to an Internet company (of all things) making Sealand the very first Internet country in the world.

All other issues pale beside the concept of using the Internet to vote. Right now fewer than 50% of us live up to our responsibilities and vote. If we could make the process of voting easier then one would expect this rate to skyrocket.

So what's keeping the vote from going online? For one thing, there is substantial controversy about this issue. Marc Strassman, writing in Spectrum, the Journal of State Government, thinks that voting on the Internet could effectively "change everything."

He says that with the legalization of Internet voting, individual voters will be empowered to vote more or less, whenever and from wherever they please. It may also become practical to allow voters to aggregate themselves in new ways rather than the current geographically-based system. This can ultimately lead to the proliferation of many new smaller parties with voters moving in and out of them at will. Says Strassman,

The need at any level for "representatives" to represent voters .... may be called into question. Direct digital democracy, the specter haunting the political landscape, may no longer hesitate to speak its own name.

Strassman says that national elites and global corporations may not find this very much to their liking which could very well be the core conflict and main story of the 21st century. As Churchill said, "Not the end, or even the beginning of the end, but perhaps the end of the beginning."

Will Internet voting make it a bit too easy? It seems that few people care about the democratic process anymore - hence the dismal voter turnout rate. The Democratic and Republican National Conventions are both television ratings disasters.

We've become a world of couch potatoes. We're tuned in (to the Internet and cable) and tuned out to politics. Many say that we spend so much time tethered to our computers, smartphones and televisions that we've become less connected to our community. How many of us even know our own neighbors?

No, we don't get much fresh air anyone. Nor do we get fresh and different perspectives. That's because if you're wired to the Internet you can ignore points of view different from yours. In essence the Internet could very well make us a nation of extremists.

It can, but it probably won't, if Internet voting is handled properly. Many people simply vote the party line and that's not likely to change even if Internet voting becomes universal. They often do this because they are completely unaware of what the other candidates stand for. Even with multi-million dollar budgets, candidate messages are not effectively relayed to the public. There is so much negative advertising that voters are left without a solid understanding of who is who.

When I first moved out of Manhattan just across the river in New Jersey I was quite unfamiliar with anything or anybody in my new hometown. A few weeks later I was asked to vote. Not knowing any of the candidates, I took the easy way out. I voted the "All politicians are crooks" line. It appealed to my warped sensibilities.

Ballot boxes and paper ballots are limited in space, but Internet ballots are not. What's to prevent the Internet voting site from providing hyperlinks to short statements of what the candidate offers?

When one shops online, particularly for hardware or software, one usually goes to a vendor's website and reads through a one page summary that lists features and benefits of that particular product. Well, a candidate is a product. He or she is offering something. These are the features. He or she has some good points that we'd all like to know about. These are the benefits.

Extremism is based on a lack of information. Internet voting has the potential to provide exactly the amount of information the voter needs to make an informed and fair decision.

@JOURNALISM

Not that long ago, the TV news program Dateline came under fierce attack for jerry-rigging a car explosion. The motives were innocent enough - to expose a safety hazard. The methodology was anything but. As a result, the Dateline disaster has become synonymous with what's wrong with journalism today.

Howard Rosenberg of the Los Angeles Times called the fiasco an "electronic Titanic - an unprecedented disaster in the annals of network news and perhaps the biggest TV scam since the Quiz scandals".

What Dateline had the audacity to do was to stage a crash test that was rigged for a particular outcome. They purposefully concealed from the public's view the hidden rockets and overfilled and loose gas tank that precipitated the crash. And if many thought the Dateline scandal was a freak or bizarre departure from accepted network standards, they were wrong. The other leading network news programs had previously run the same sorts of grossly misleading crash videos and simulations, while also withholding material facts about the tests.

Perhaps the most serious of misjudgments on Dateline's part was in trusting "experts" who were deeply involved in litigating against the target of the expose.

The June 1993 issue of National Review focuses on one salient topic: "The Decline of American Journalism. Although the publication has a bias admittedly right of center, the 40-odd pages devoted to this topic were rare in their self-exposure for the early 1990s. The basic message of this series of articles is that journalists themselves are biased, and that they write through the haze of their bias. In other words, since most journalists are quite liberal in their political stance, liberal causes are usually written about supportively while conservative topics (i.e. immigration reform) are written about less enthusiastically - if at all. Those astute readers who have noticed the seemingly ironclad embrace of the "politically correct" movement by the press will understand immediately what I am referring to.

Criticism of the press is not limited to right-ofcenter publications. A literature search on the subject turns up these gems,

Junk stories are slowly eroding the public's faith in the media. The press is being used as dupes for lawyers and other charlatans who want to implicate public figures. Seeking to satisfy what they perceive to be the tastes of the American public, the press is printing first and asking questions later.

It seems that the love affair with the media is just about over, although not everyone appears to have gotten the message. Press people have as many foibles and prejudices as the rest of us. They make errors. They take shortcuts.

Unfortunately, somewhere around third grade or so, it was hammered into us that the printed word was "gospel." Hit's in writing, it must be so we learned. This is a habit that's hard to break.

Ira Stoll considers himself an ordinary, semi-intelligent guy. But he's from Brooklyn so he's got an attitude and that attitude tells him that there's something rotten in the state of Denmark - or the New York Times, to be precise.

He reads the Times every day and every day he finds errors of fact and logic so he decided to do something about it. That something was to create a web site called smartertimes.com. smartertimes is just that - a smarter version of the New York Times.

The most interesting thing about smartertimes.com is that Stoll attempts to be impartial and discuss both sides of a particular issues - something that the traditionally liberal media does not do. For example, Stoll once blasted the Times for reporting that Cuba's medical system - although beleaguered by shortages - has been praised by some experts as a model for community and preventative medicine. Stoll retorted, "The Cuban public health successes are like the Soviet Union's agricultural successes - the imaginary creations of Communist bureaucrats whose career advancement depends on creating statistics to demonstrate successes even when the reality is that of miserable failure."

Smartertimes and Stoll are even willing to tackle "sacred cows" - issues on race and immigration - which are almost never discussed critically within the media. Stoll caustically discusses a New York Times article which applauds as a success story the Boston police department because the proportion of blacks in uniform there approximates the proportion of black residents in the city. According to the New York Times article,

The force's integration success comes from the proposition that something approaching racial balancing -- a police force whose demographics match those of the city -- can improve not just the social climate but the effectiveness of the police as well.

Stoll's rebuttal echoes the non-verbalized sentiments of a goodly proportion of Times readers,

Imagine if these standards were applied to Jews in college

admissions. Would the Times judge it a success story if the proportion of Jews in Ivy league colleges approximated the proportion of Jewish residents in America .... Or suppose the National Basketball Association suddenly decided that it was going to fill its teams by racial balancing.

A significant number of readers think that the media is biased - one way or the other - although traditionally people going into this line of work appear to be liberal in orientation.

Bias manifests itself in several ways. One way is to publish articles that continually tout a particular perspective and the other is to derail the publication of any articles discussing "the other side of the issue". Both Queens, New York and Bergen County in New Jersey have had an influx of immigrants over the last few decades. The regional newspapers, Newsday Queens edition and The Record respectively, frequently publish articles touting the benefits of immigration. So many are published that more than one person interviewed for this book wondered out loud whether the goal of all this positive spin was brainwashing.

In January of 1999 thirteen journalists were brought together to discuss why there has been a profound shift in journalism from straight news to editorialized news,

Two imperatives in contemporary journalism are at war with one another. One imperative says: be smart! Be analytic! .... The other imperative says: Don 't say anything that will make your readers - or, more important, your sources mad.

The sums up rather nicely what seems to pass for much of journalism today - "don't make people mad".

This group of 13 discusses an even more serious problem that seems to pervade the hallowed halls of the print and broadcasting media today - the problem of self-referential journalism.

It 's a kind of journalism of nihilism - it doesn't believe in anything

except itself Journalism has become, to an astonishing degree, self-referential, like a tribe cut off from the rest of the world. When Maureen Dowd, the current queen of the tribe, and others of her ilk sneer at those who would like to see a journalism that actually cares about things the country cares about, that's when their cards are most on the table ..... Note, also, by the way, how the only people she ever quotes in her Ain't-I-One-Smart-Cookie op-ed columns are her fellow journalists.

Our tribe of 13 goes on to discuss a wide variety of problems such as the fact that today's famous journalists spend too much time spitting out opinions and predictions rather than taking in new material, to an over dependence on the "sex sells" type of news all to frequently dominates the headlines today.

Transparencynow.com is an interesting web site edited by an old-hand writer, columnist and editor who's appeared in the Boston Globe, the Nation and Newsday. Ken Sanes started the site to offer up his 24 years of expertise on the subject. Online since 1997, Transparencynow has been described by the Institut Universitari de l'Audiovisual in Barteclona as "a magnificent theoretical area which contains a careful selection of critiques of the mass media, politics and popular culture". Channel One Network describes Transparency as "a remarkable web site that is full of thoughtful essays about the challenges and delights of living in a media saturated society".

In the Transparency article, "The News Media's Effort to Hide from Significant Truth", Sanes talks about the psychology of journalism. He mentions Freud's discovery that we are enslaved by illusion - that we misperceive the events of adult life in terms of our childhood fears and desires. Freud argued that it was the ability to see the truth that had the power to free us from illusion. Sanes then goes on to quote Gandhi's philosophy that we have to break the cycle of deception and violence that is inflicted on each generation by the one before, which results in the distortions of neurosis.

Sanes combines these two philosophies into one that is all important for journalists - that those who fight for liberating truth [journalists] cannot become enmeshed in the cycle of untruth and violence that they are trying to break. Instead, journalists need to stand outside the cycle of violence, corruption and manipulated information that makes up the power relations of society with the goal of showing readers the truth of the system and how it works. Unfortunately, Sanes says, journalists are themselves immersed in this system of untruth,

Like other players in this system, they engage in symbolic violence against reputations; they manipulate information to achieve various ends; they make covert alliances, and offer the public forms of untruth that masquerade as truth. And they do so even as they depict themselves as honest brokers who stand outside the system and expose its flaws to public scrutiny.

Sanes goes on to say that journalists have very much become a part of this corruption. Most decision making in America as well as other nations is, for the most part, under the control of a kind or virtual oligarchy which is made up of corporations, political groups and the media. All of these manipulate the government to achieve their own ends and use the mass media to shape public opinion.

So, the question is, wherein lies the truth?

The American Society of Magazine Editors has a rule which prohibits advertisements with an editorial appearance. This role is regularly broken, particularly in trade magazines. But it's also broken in the traditional media. I regularly see fashion advertorials disguised as the fashion pages of the New York Times Magazine. One of the most early examples of this form of adjournalism was on the cover of the now defunct Nevada Woman magazine. It seemed harmless enough - an article about the "Women of Wells Fargo." The problem was that Wells Fargo paid for it.

Paige Fleming, the chief executive and publisher of Nevada Woman said that, while they'd draw the line at allowing political candidates to pay for covers, she saw nothing wrong with the Wells Fargo deal. She also said that she did not think it was necessary to let readers know about the sponsorships. How odd because even her client, Wells Fargo, insisted that "readers should always be fully informed of the difference between editorial content and advertising in the media".

At a certain point, people won't be able to differentiate between what's trustworthy and what isn't, says Orville Schell, Dean of the Graduate School of Journalism at the University of California at Berkeley. Over the long term, he worries, this loss of credibility could have a corrosive effect on society in general - especially given the media's importance as a political, cultural and economic watchdog. "If people don't trust their information, it's not much better than a Marxist-Leninist society.

It got so bad that the Federal Trade Commission issued an Enforcement Policy Statement on Deceptively in 2015.

One of the biggest criticisms of the media is that they seem to write for people that just don't exist. In the Spring and Summer of 2001 the public was inundated with 24x7 news about Chandra Levy. Levy is the intern that disappeared. Her disappearance, while newsworthy, was not what made her primetime. What made her eminently newsworthy was her relationship with Representative Gary Condit. From the relentless coverage of this story one would get the impression that Americans are sensation-seeking morons swigging beer and salivating over allegations of sexual wrong-doing. The fact is that most Americans are completely disinterested in the Chandra Levy story.

A nationwide survey by the Pew Research Center for the People and the Press finds only 16% of Americans very interested in the story.

According to Andrew Kohut, a director at Pew, most Americans blanch at the blatant exploitation of the people being covered, and they indicate in surveys that they feel the press pursues these stories to enlarge audiences. Kohut questions the wisdom of alienating a large percentage of a public that now has the ability to screen out the news it does not want by turning to the Internet.

So the question becomes, is the Internet a better place to get the news? Certainly, the Internet affords more avenues to get the news. It is possible to get the news whenever you want and from wherever you want. If you live in New York City you are generally limited to getting local and some national and international headline news from your local papers, radio and TV stations. On the Internet, alternatively, you can tune in to - say - Phoenix local news and find out what's going on there from a native's perspective. From a business person's perspective this provides a major competitive advantage over traditional media. If you want to do business in Phoenix it is critical to understand the business climate in this particular location. The New York Times just won't cut the mustard for this particular task.

The beginning of this chapter talked at great length about the bias of the traditional media and how they take it upon themselves to determine just which news the public will hear and which news they won't. The Internet, on the other hand, provides the opportunity for all news to be heard.

Matt Drudge, more than anyone else, turned online journalism into a force to be reckoned with. Drudge, if you didn't know, was the one that leaked the Monica Lewinsky story. Traditional media absolutely hate Matt. Critics charge that he has no time to know his sources or check his facts. They say he embodies the most dangerous aspects of online journalism, where a conspiracy theory can move the stock market of a stained blue dress can almost destroy a presidency.

No matter the criticisms, Matt is interesting. And he's no

worse than most journalists (Deep Throat, anyone?),

We have entered an era vibrating with the din of small voices. Every citizen can be a reporter, can take on the powers that be. The difference between the Internet, television and radio, magazines and newspapers is the two-way communication. The Net gives as much voice to .... me as to a CEO or speaker of the house. We all become equal.

Drudge has a tendency to among the first to report on political topics. This morning I am editing this chapter amid a barrage of news on the impeachment proceedings against President Donald Trump, a purveyor and complainer of fake news himself. As usual, the Drudge Report is right on the money.

Lawmakers could draft articles of impeachment by end of October... White House Knew of Whistleblower Allegations Soon After Trump Call With Ukraine Leader...Acted to 'lock down' record...STORED ON SEPARATE COMPUTER NETWORK.. Part of broader secrecy effort...COMPLAINT ALLEGES COVER-UP...Trump Alludes to Punishment for White House Spies...VIDEO..Transcript...Dems charge witness intimidation...NYT: IT'S A CIA OFFICER...
TURN: 2 Republican governors support impeachment....WEST WING 'SHELL-SHOCKED'...Pence in spotlight...RUDY: When this is over, I will be the hero...Giuliani engaged parade of Ukrainian prosecutors...America filled with anger and animosity digs in...Only the ballot box will deliver final verdict!

Drudge's type of reporting is quite interactive. He says that most of his sources are concerned citizens, in and out of government. That he takes these leads and runs with them is a testament to his value as a reporter. He appears to understand what is newsworthy.

I used to live in the town of Edgewater in the state of New Jersey. Edgewater, which has a fabulous view of the New York skyline, was a town in decline in the early 1990s.

Industry moved out of town and the waterfront was barren and occasionally toxic. To get developers to clean-up and then build on the waterfront the Mayor rescinded rent control. Unfortunately for the new tenants this little bit of information was never shared with anyone. Prospective tenants who called the town to find out whether there was rent control were given - knowingly or unknowingly - misinformation. So in they moved.

In the early 2000s the New York City real estate market experienced a seismic boom. In the rental market, aided and abetted by the very Republican George Pataki, many of the tenant protections were repealed. The New York City rental market is one of the most expensive in the nation. A nice two bedroom goes for upwards of $4000. This means that only the rich and the subsidized poor can live in the City making New York a lot duller without the writers and artists who can no longer afford to live there. Worse, teachers and other public servants have long commutes to get to and from their jobs.

In 1995, Pataki's team voted in something called vacancy decontrol (thankfully repealed in 2019). What this means is that when a rent controlled or stabilized apartment is vacated the landlord can raise it to market rates - which is usually unaffordable for most people.

Once the rates rose to stratospheric levels in Manhattan folks started moving to the close-in burbs including Edgewater. Rents in this town have edged upwards of $3,000 for a two-bedroom apartment. Unfortunately, without rent control greedy landlords usually take advantage of their tenants. One complex, now owned by the California Teacher's Retirement System, did just this. They raised rents upwards of $4000 per month.

Outraged, the local paper was called (The Bergen Record). Not only was this a fabulous human interest story, but it would be a public service to warn current residents of Edgewater about their impending financial peril. Did the Bergen Record report on this story? No, they didn't. Instead they ran a delightful story about the Mock Parrots of Edgewater aptly demonstrating the provincialism of the local media and their inability to understand what is actually newsworthy.

Online journalists can be fast on the uptake. Sometimes too fast for both the traditional media and those they write about. Hillary Clinton says,

We're all going to have to rethink how we deal with the Internet. As exciting as these new developments are, there are a number of serious issues without any kind of editing function or gatekeeping function .... Any time an individual leaps so far ahead of that balance and throws the system, whatever it might be - political, economic, technological out of balance, you've got a problem. It can lead to all kinds of bad outcomes which we have seen historically.

Hilllary lived the truth of her words during the 2016 election when various right-wing news sites such as Breitbart and FoxNews, aided and abetted by Facebook and the Russians, distorted the election news cycle.

In June 2001, Michael Kinsley, then editor of Slate.com admitted that he'd been the victim of a hoax. Writer Jay Forman turned out to have fabricated every important element of a story in which he claimed to have gone "monkeyfishing" - using fishing poles to catch monkeys in the Florida keys.

Of course, anyone with a brain in their heads would disbelieve a story as ridiculous as this. The hoax only came to light when the New York Times debunked the story and Kinsley finally owned up to the fact that perhaps Slate.com had some fine-tuning to do when it came to fact checking.

Unfortunately, the online press suffers from the same foibles as the traditional press. This is understandable given that today, much of the online press, is run by the traditional press.

ABC, NBC, the New York Times, MSNBC all run extensive online operations. Their sites are large, dynamic and contain lots of ads. Sometimes, however, these ads cross an important boundary - that between advertising and editorial. Forbes.com is an example. It has run ads for Microsoft that could easily be mistaken for staff-written articles. Quite a few media companies have taken a step down this slippery slope. In 1999 General Electric, which originally the CNBC news channel and web site, took a stake in Archipeligo Holdings.

Archipeligo is a communications network for trading stocks - a bit of a conflict of interest for a supposedly impartial financial news service. Since the dot-crash in 2000, and the financial crisis in 2008, it's been a challenge for many dot-coms to achieve profitability (gobs of venture capital funding aside – I mean you WeWork) - particularly those that offer content (e.g. news). Since charging readers subscription fees has been somewhat of a failure, and most forms of advertising have had dismal results leading to heated debates over the virtues of click-through (advertisers' side) versus branding (publishers' side), publishers have desperately sought a new model to support their operations.

The model of the moment appears to be e-commerce transaction fees. This shift in the way the media make their money could potentially affect the way they cover the news. If Ford is partnering with a particular media web site to sell its wares, then that media site might think twice before criticizing Ford. Think about the ramifications if the media had not exposed the FordlFirestore tire blowout story. It could happen.

Worse is the possibility that the media might be seduced into keeping their "business partners" happy by puffing up their coverage of that particular product and covering up defects in that product. CBS decided not to broadcast a bunch of "Family Law" reruns after Procter & Gamble threatened to withdraw its commercials. This is a particularly worrisome example of the tastes of a large advertiser influencing the network's programming decisions.

ABC, now owned by Disney, already does this. I can't count how many "specials" I've seen advertised which, when viewed, are actually thinly disguised promos for Disney movies. When the cartoon Atlantis was ready to be released, ABC ran a special about the secrets of Atlantis. Now this is right up my alley. From the advertisements for the special I assumed (stupidly) that it was going to be somewhat akin to the more scientific programs that now appear on the Discovery or Learning channels. Instead the "special" was really a trailer for the cartoon. I had been duped.

This sort of questionable integrity goes on all the time. When Amazon.com was found to be taking fees of up to $10,000 for books that it labeled as "destined for greatness" its customers were outraged and the practice stopped dead in its tracks. The key here was that the customers found out. What if the customers had not found out?

I go to book stores all the time. I often stand at the end of a row of books and skim though these books that seem to occupy a special place in the bookstore. Books placed in prominent positions on tables or at the ends of the aisles would appear to be somehow more important or better than the books stacked knee deep on the shelves. I discovered otherwise when my then publisher, McGrawHill, paid $10,000 for my book on web casting to sit at the end of the aisle at Barnes and Noble stores (heck I would have stood outside my local B&N store and hawked the book for that 10 grand). Was my book on webcasting better than other books on the same topic that could be found on the shelves? Probably not, but to casual browsers it would appear to be.

On the Internet the deal between publisher and client is much more less obvious than in traditional advertising. It's much harder to discern whether that glowing article about XYZ company isn't the result of a relationship between the XYZ company and the publisher. But then again, it's always been this way. As an audience, the public has just been very naive. As John Swinton, an editor at the New York Times, and deceased in 1901, once said,

There is no such thing, at this date of the world's history, in America, as an independent press. You know it and I know it. There is not one of you who dares to write your honest opinions, and if you did, you know beforehand that it would never appear in print.. ... The business of the journalists is to destroy the truth, to lie outright, to pervert, to vilify, to fawn at the feet of mammon .... We are the tools and vassals of rich men behind the scenes. We are the jumping jacks, they pull the strings and we dance ..... We are intellectual prostitutes.

So we've been duped from the beginning, we just didn't know it. Mickey Kaus (twitter.com/kausmickey), a former writer for Newsweek and the New Republic, understood this and finally had to throw in the towel. He wanted to write the truth, damnit!

Kaus does this via Twitter. He has this to say about whether he could write the pithy articles he does now for the traditional media,

Off the top of my head, no I couldn't. They wouldn't let me get down to this level of detail and personal obsession. By the time I wrote half of it, it would be obsolete - certainly by the time it was edited and printed. When I wrote a weekly column, about a third of the effort was coming up with a topic that would hold up until the publication date. That's no longer a worry. I don't have to worry about getting things past my editors, since I have no editors - or rather I edit myself. Even at the New Republic there were some things I couldn't say. I also do a lot of research by email, which lets me turn out things faster, plus readers send in tips and critiques by e-mail .... .I don't have to cover things I'm not interested in and I can get to the point quicker.

Old-hand journalists like Kaus and new ones like Matt Drudge deliver the type of content you simply can't find anywhere else. Much of this new form of journalism examines issues from both sides - something that the traditional media are not wont to do.

The new e- journalism also goes one or two better than traditional journalism by putting to use the full power of technology. In 1999 22-year old Amadou Diallo was shot at by the New York City police 41 times. Nineteen bullets struck the unarmed man. While news media provided extensive coverage of the story, one web site offered a whole lot more.

APBnews.net partnered with Columbia University Journalism and Computer Science departments to provide what they call a "contextual view of the killing". Using a camera invented by a Columbia University professor of Computer Science which shoots a 360-degree view, this high-tech news team was able to photograph both the vestibule of Diallo's apartment as well as the street where he lived. Those who visited the APBnews.com site were able to examine the street and apartment, panning, tilting or zooming anywhere in the entire field of view. Essentially, you were able "see" through the eyes of the victim.

This interactivity not only provides more context for the events of that evening, but can engage the audience in ways not possible in the world of traditional journalism. Many believe that this is critically important for journalism in the 21st century.

The advent of the smartphone camera has made all of us journalists. Many news stations accept photos and videos through their citizen apps. Even without sending your sensational video to the news media, just posting the photo or video to Facebook might lead to it becoming viral.

Unfortunately, it's sometimes hard to find the wheat for all the chafe on the Web. There are millions of sites and while Drudge's name became famous because of Monica's stained blue dress it's rather hard to distinguish the nutcases from the legitimate journalists. I just happened on Mickey Kaus' site. But for every reputable site like Kaus' there are one or more disreputable sites.

For the most part this wealth of sites, sometimes run more as hobbies than as businesses, illustrates how the Internet provides an open market of ideas and breaks down many of the natural barriers that previously enabled editors to dictate what would be the news of any particular day.

Our friend Mickey Kaus, ex-newsman extraordinaire, is representative of that new breed of solo pundit that airs his or her opinions online in a sort of me-zine format. Working in grungy shorts, jeans or sweats, these folks work alone, at odd hours and often have odd opinions. While more than a few of them are the garden-variety of e-neighborhood crank a growing handful, like Kaus, are professional writers trying to break free of the constraints of professional journalism.

Alas, no one is really making a penny out of these "spill your guts" web sites. Then again, few online publications are making any money. This has led some to start charging (gasp) subscription fees. I know I won't dig into my change purse to read something that used to be free (sorry). And I'm not alone. According to a survey by the Consumer Electronics Association, 77 percent of respondents opposed paying any fees for "commodity" information, such as online news, driving directions and financial reports. The future of online content is, it would seem, rather murky,

These new me-zines are also not without critics. Some say that they're one-person vanity presses. They often contain a lot of pontification without real reporting to back up the opinions.

Andrew Sullivan, of andrewsullivan.com and a former editor at the New Republic and writer for New York Magazine, counters that his readers understand his role as an opinionated filter. "They know my job is to read everything I can and get irritated as much as I can and sputter for them on a daily basis".

All this sputter makes for interesting reading and a lot more readers. So much so that the "majors" are borrowing a page from these start-ups. Even the esteemed Wall Street Journal at one point started a "Heard on the Net" column.

As Sullivan puts it, "the ego has landed."

@WORK

When my friends commiserate with each other over the rather lousy job situation today they like to talk about their fathers. Dad, they say, had an unwritten contract with his employer. He'd get to work for 25 or so years and they would never think of laying him off. He had job security.

Most of our dads, in fact, did have only one job for most of their careers. I know mine did. Dad worked for CIT Financial in New York City for several decades, after stints in the army, college and as a tour-bus hawker in Times Square during the '40s. He moved slowly, but surely, up the corporate later and finally, late in his career, actually became an officer of the company. When he retired they gave him a party, a watch and a pension and that was that.

Today most of us have anywhere from five to seven jobs during a career punctuated by layoffs, resignations, the gig economy and generally not very good times. But it's a fantasy to think that all of our Dads and Granddads really had it any better.

One need only look at great literature for a record of what the "olden days" was really like. Charles Dickens painfully vivid description of being poor in the London of *Oliver Twist* to Upton Sinclair's sensational account of what work life was like for meatpacking workers in (1906) *The Jungle.* Both books provoked public outrage. In fact, President Theodore Roosevelt was so horrified by Sinclair's depiction of workplace amputations, lacerations and other injuries that he launched a federal inquiry into the practices of Chicago's meatpacking industry. It wasn't until after World War II, however, that the meatpackers' union finally gave the workers in this industry what they fought so hard for - a middle class existence.

Eric Schlosser in his very fine book *Fast Food Nation* deconstructs how the meatpacking industry went from using high-paid skilled labor to largely unskilled, migrant labor in just a few short decades. The cause, according to Schlosser was McDonalds,

They have turned one of the nation's best-paying manufacturing jobs into one of the lowest-paying, created a migrant industrial workforce of poor immigrants, tolerated high injury rates, and spawned rural ghettos in the American heartland.

Once upon a time in America everyone who could afford to ate out in restaurants. When the national highway system was built and automobile travel became ubiquitous, fast food restaurants were born to service these now car-loving Americans. Back then, however, fast food meant car hops, short order cooks and a varied menu. If you're old enough you might remember the short-skirted girls on roller skates who took your order, everyone else is invited to rent the now legendary movie *American Graffiti* to get a feel for the era. All those girls and short order cooks were expensive for the owners of these first fast food establishments.

Taking a cue from the assembly lines of automobile manufacturing, the fast food industry now automates and standardizes practically every facet of the business. Skilled labor need no longer apply. Instead the fast food workforce is made up almost entirely of people under 20, and a smattering of oldsters.

The strict regimentation at fast food restaurants creates standardized products. It increases the throughput, And it gives fast food companies an enormous amount of power over their employees. When management determines exactly how every task is to be done .... and can impose its own rules about pace, output, quality and technique, it makes workers increasingly interchangeable. The management no longer depends upon the talents of skills of its workers .... Jobs that have been de-skilled can be filled cheaply. The need to retain any individual worker is greatly reduced by the ease with which he or she can be replaced.

As the fast food industry began to consolidate to a very few, very large players (i.e. McDonalds, Burger King, etc.) they decided that they needed to call the shots beyond their own restaurant doors. They now wanted to call the shots in the meatpacking industry. Dictating what, how and where they also decided to reduce the number of meatpacking firms they would work with. The ones chosen ultimately became meatpacking industry powerhouses.

In 1960 two former Swift & Company executives decided to start their own meatpacking company to compete with these giants. But it couldn't be business as usual. They need to dramatically reduce production costs to stay in the game. To do so they decided to apply the same techniques used at McDonald's - eliminate skilled labor. Using a combination of technology, new procedures and cheap immigrant labor, they did just this. Not only did they successfully achieve their goal of reducing costs they created a whole new way of packaging meat. Instead of shipping whole sides of beef, they now shipped smaller cuts, vacuum-sealed or plastic-packed. This new marketing technique virtually eliminated the need for skilled butchers in grocery stores as well.

Meatpacking isn't the only industry to be "modernized" by technology plus low-skilled labor. Farm owners are also using this combination to reduce costs. Of course, a byproduct of these techniques is to reduce the demand for domestic workers.

Like the meatpacking industry, growers much prefer newly arrived immigrants. In fact, the government has a program which enables farmers to import thousands of workers on H-2A visas to harvest crops. Presumably this vast number is a result of a severe labor shortage. But is this really true?

Study after study of the H-2A program concludes that there's really a surplus of agricultural labor, not a shortage. Unemployment and underemployment are endemic among farmworkers. In studies and congressional testimony about the program, the General Accounting Office also dismisses the idea of a labor shortage. Agricultural employers in most of the United States have had adequate supplies of labor for many years and continue to do so, the GAO reports ..... The H2-A program has, in effect, turned NAFTA inside out: Since U.S. farms can't go to the Third World, the federal government lets agribusiness bring the Third World to U.S. farms.

So here we have it again, unskilled labor + technology = McDonaldization. Of course, this formula is not limited to meatpacking and agriculture. A variation of McDonaldization has been creeping its way into industry since the formula was created.

In my father's day, skilled workers all had the same expectations. They started out, in their twenties, as junior staffers and gradually worked their way up the ranks. No 20-something bosses here. You first had to pay your dues, and gather some experience.

Pre-Internet technology started the ball rolling. When I started my first professional job most executives had private secretaries. Everyone else shared one or two secretaries. These were the folks that typed and mailed your letters and interoffice memos. In 1981 there was a sea change. The personal computer was introduced to office workers. Along with the hardware came a couple of revolutionary software packages including a word processor and spreadsheet. Over time, most office workers started doing their own typing gradually reducing the need for a large pool of typists and secretarial staff.

Over the next two decades great strides were made and we saw the rise of complex, sophisticated "thinking" technologies such as expert systems, neural networks and machine learning. While we are nowhere close to the wonders seen in Steven Spielberg's movie "Artificial Intelligence" we do have software today that can predict the behavior of consumers, diagnose software problems, act as your virtual receptionist and even drive cars (somewhat.) Elimination by technology, it seems, is moving up the food chain.

Technology, globalization and a bouncing ball economy have changed the dynamics of being an employee. In Europe the unemployment rate hovers around 7.5%, although there are vast variations between individual

countries - up to 13.9% unemployment in Spain. In the United States the government will only admit to a 3.7% unemployment rate but most of us know otherwise. If you add in those that fall off the unemployment rolls (and are therefore not counted in the official statistics) and add in underemployed workers such as part-timers who really want full time jobs, then the real unemployment rate has been calculated to be as high as 7.3%.

Technological advances coupled with cheap labor overseas have further diminished the opportunities for American workers in several ways. When was the last time you called an 800 number for help? You might be surprised to find that a goodly number of folks that you are talking to are thousands of miles away. That sweet woman with the Midwest accent on the other end of the phone just might be sitting in a massive call center somewhere in India. If you should strike up a conversation and ask her where she hails from her instructions would be to fib a bit and mention some American city.

My own industry - technology - seems to have put this formula into high gear. Dr. Norman Matloff of the University of California at Davis provided extensive testimony to the U.S. House Judiciary Committee Subcommittee on Immigration on why software labor shortage, touted as critical by the industry and its organizations, was purely a myth.

Most of the major players in the industry, along with a leading trade group, are perennially pleading with Congress to raise the number of foreign guest workers allowed under the Hl-B visa program. In spite of testimony which negated the misrepresentations of the Information Technology Association of America (ITAA), Congress opens the floodgates and permits employers to import tens of thousands of programmers to the U.S. each year.

Readers of the articles proclaiming a shortage would be perplexed if they also knew that Microsoft only hires 2% of its applicants for software positions, and that this rate is typical in the industry. Software employers, large and small, across the nation, concede that they receive huge numbers of resumes but reject most of them without even an interview. One does not have to be a "techie" to see the contradiction here. A 2% hiring rate might be unremarkable in other fields, but not in one in which there is supposed to be a "desperate" labor shortage. If employers were that desperate, they would certainly not be hiring just a miniscule fraction of their job applicants.

What these companies are really after is cheap labor. There are several ways of accomplishing this. You can hire directly from universities. In this way you get young people with good skills who are open to lower salaries just to get in the door, although starting salaries are creeping up. If you walked through the hallways of any number of tech companies you might have noticed the "youngness" of the personnel - from the

CEO down to the programmers.

These kids live and breathe their jobs. They glide right from the dorm to the office which if often made-up to look like a typical dorm - complete with pizza, beer and basketball hoops. In fact, it is not atypical for one of these tech kiddies not to have a life at all. Often spending 80 or more hours a week at the job, it is just not possible for any sort of social life outside of work. Hence, work and private life merge. Once an employee burns out, and this happens often, it is rather easy to replace that worker with yet another up and coming fresh-faced, eager-to-please college grad.

A second, and even cheaper way, to get workers is via the H1-B program. Guest workers, often from India or China, could be secured at rates often below the market rate. Interestingly, this is not just a US-based phenomenon.

Declaring that "Germany needs immigrants", a high-level commission urged the nation to admit tens of thousands of skilled foreign workers every year to help offset an aging, shrinking population. The report suggested issuing long-term work permits to up to 50,000 young foreigners a year, including allowing permanent residence for 20,000 highly trained workers. Another 20,000 would be allowed to fill shorter-term vacancies in growing fields such as software programming and 10,000 others would be offered trainee visas ..... At the same time the German Chancellor hopes to keep resentment among ....jobless Germans in check.

There seems to be a bit of a contradiction here. I am presuming that at least some of the jobless Germans are capable of being trained for these skilled jobs, particularly since some of this quota would allow for up to 10,000 trainee visas.

Perhaps the most cost-effective technique for saving money, however damaging to U.S.-based workers, is to build a "software development center" overseas,

Teaneck, July 4,2001 - Cognizant Technology Solutions Corp., a software developer that said in November it would spend $30 million over two years in India, plans to build three development centers in the Asian nation, as more U.S. companies move their [software development] operations overseas. The complexes will eventually employ more than 6.500 workers and total 600,000 square feet .... More than two-thirds of Cognizant's current 3,500 employees work in India.

More and more companies are outsourcing their software operations overseas. Ireland is another popular location. In all of these places, the labor is talented, eager and most importantly cheaper.

Of course, industry leaders will never own up to their "cheaper is better" call to arms. They cover their tracks by stating that there's not enough skilled workers to go around or that those that are available simply do not have the requisite important skills.

This last "requirement" is what lets the tech industry (as well as other industries) avoid hiring older workers. Most people I speak to seem to be brainwashed (by the industry) into believing that programmers with many years of experience in one programming language just can't cut the mustard and learn a new "hot" programming language such as Java.

This is, of course, a lot of nonsense. It's the science of engineering that's hard to learn - the methodologies behind analysis, design, testing and implementation. Programming languages are actually a dime a dozen. Once you understand how to program in one language, it is fairly easy to pick up a second, third, fourth or even fifth programming language.

The real truth is that hiring an older programmer is just much more expensive than a younger programmer and/or importing a foreign worker and/or exporting it all overseas.

Age discrimination is rampant in this field, starting even as young as 35. Though industry lobbyists like to dismiss this as being supported only by anecdotal evidence, the fact is that there is a plethora of hard data which show that older programmers and engineers do face major difficulties in finding programming and engineering job.

Matloff quotes some interesting statistics such as: it takes three more weeks for a laid-off programmer or engineer to find a job for each year of age; a survey of hiring managers found that only 2% of them would prefer to hire an applicant with more than 10 years of experience.

My own experience tells me that Matloff's statistics are on target. My nephew is a high-tech recruiter. He tells me that most of his clients tell him not to even bother sending a resume of someone older than 40!

In a vain attempt to compete with the young and the foreign, many older workers go the retraining route. This, according to Matloff, doesn't seem to work either as the employers state that what they really want is training plus experience. Interestingly, these employers don't seem to mind the fact that most college graduates also have no "real experience" either. In addition, more than one employer has found that the experience-level of their H1- B importees is not quite what they were hoping for. After all, you can put anything on a resume. But these employers are not complaining. They really don't mind too much on-the-job training - if the employee's salary is low enough!

I am 49 years old and a graduate of Lafayette College with a BS in EE and a 3.1 average. I was a part time student working full time with travel, and a student at night. I have also been unemployed for over a year. Prior to my unemployment, I was a software writer for a British CAD/CAM company (RADAN CIM). Last year they shut down the main United States office in Philadelphia and laid everyone off (US employees). Since the son of the owner lived in

California, the board elected to move the office to California and staff it with HlBs from England. They would work for half of our salary and were given a car and rooms at company expense. Since then I have applied everywhere and been told that I have no useful skills .. .I also passed the state exam for professional engineers (EIT) but that doesn't help. I have been told by head hunters that unless I made $100,000 a year or were a manager that I have no value to society, that I was a failure. When I went to the Lafayette College Career Center, the woman there just opened her book and said you should expect $50,000 /yr and here are some books you should read ... The state of Pennsylvania sent me a letter after my unemployment ran out saying I needed to be retrained. They thought truck driving school could be a new career. Yes, they knew I was a recent grad. I don't think I am special in the treatment I am receiving however in this booming economy I have sent out about 200 resumes from electronic tech to starting software writer and have only received one reply. That was as a drill press operator. Either Lafayette College is a trash school or the age discrimination is larger than anyone believes .

Ageism has always been a problem, albeit not such a blatant one. Even during the era of "unwritten guarantee of a lifelong job" there were some problems. I remember the 1974 Jack Lemmon movie, "The Prisoner of Second Avenue". In this serio-comedy a man loses his job in an ad agency after 22 years. He suspects his age has something to do with it as well as his inability to find a new job. And this was close to three decades ago.

Back in the seventies, however, experience was actually valued.

Aside from a rather "detrimental to society" emphasis on youth culture to the point of lunacy on television and in the movies, technology changed. All through this section I've been trying to make a case for my theory that:

inexperienced workers + technology + cheap wages = one

happy employer

When I learned how to write a program the art of programming was hard stuff. We didn't have too many tools to help us write and debug the code and generate and then package the executables. While I agree that today's Java, C++/ etc. programming languages are far more sophisticated than, say, COBOL, these languages are on par with the complexity of my first language, which was Assembler. So, in effect, technology has made programming more straight-forward enabling employers to hire less-experienced employees.

Today's program development toolsets make simple work of much of the laborious effort of programming. In fact, the real value of the object-oriented languages (i.e. Python, Java and C++) was supposed to be that you can effectively glue a series of reusable objects together quickly to make a brand new program. The whole purpose behind OOP was/is reusability. So it is quite possible to hire some skilled but inexperienced workers, throw some tools at them and get the required productivity.

Many of the out of work whiners are Java programmers, ASP people, Flash developers, etc. Not real computer professionals. Front end development was never very difficult, and now has become so simple that body shops can fill the needs of most corporations for about 15 dollars an hour. It would seem tragic, but when you think that all that's necessary to "attain" expertise in any of the tools you might find on your typical e-commerce resume is a 40 dollar book from Amazon, you can see that a general deflation in salary is in order.

Where does this leave the experienced worker? Angry and posting messages on various Internet bulletin boards, one of which posts this introductory message,

As we were growing up, we knew that at some time in the future, we would retire and go on to live the good life based on our work efforts and health. Computers have changed that paradigm ....

Most say that they are being completely overlooked

because employers expect them to ask for the same salary that they received before.

To discount an applicant solely due to his/her previous compensation levels should be a thing of the past, writes Robert Puntney of Apple River,Illinois who lost his job 17 months ago. Most 40-plus unemployed folks I've talked to ... don't expect to receive the same salary they once commanded. Considering a 30% - 50% reduction in salary to be able to utilize one's experience and skill set within a challenging atmosphere is quickly becoming the norm rather than the exception for the 40-plus white-collar worker.

Of course, youth culture-obsessed age discrimination is not always technology dependent as demonstrated by the many high profile age discrimination class action suit against TV networks, studios, production companies and talent agencies. The U.S. Equal Employment Commission' says that age discrimination is a persistent problem with more than 16,000 age discrimination complaints are filed each year, with disastrous financial consequences for the person affected.

Perhaps no one has fallen on harder times than 56-year old Tracy Keenan Wynn, who wrote scripts like "The Autobiography of Miss Jane Pittman", "The Longest Yard" and "Tribes" and received Emmy and Writers Guild awards along the way. Wynn hasn't found steady work since 1997 and currently house-sits for a friend in Aspen, the Colorado ski resort town. His wealth melted away in recent years. Wynn watched $150,000 in stocks and bonds evaporate and lost his home, cash and belongings when he filed for bankruptcy.

Work has indeed changed, and because of the Internet we can gripe about our problems anytime, day or night. When the dot-coms started to go dot-bust in the early part of this century, a clever young man started a web site with a name sure to offend. Fuckedcompany.com, the self-proclaimed dead pool of the Internet industry, cataloged 20- and 30-something career angst in real time. Industry rumors, usually concerning the demise or imminent demise of a dot-com company, are posted and participants are encouraged to post comments (usually profane).

Although you have to sift through what the owner, whose name is Pud, rightly calls "crap", a quick tour through the site gives some good indication of the reality of working in this brave new world.

I think the thrill is gone. For most people the dotcom implosion is beginning to really hit home as an annihilation of a career, loss of hope and the reality of an economically unstable future. It's not so funny when half the people you know have been canned, can't pay the rent and are eating another box of Mac and Cheese.

Another anonymous poster describes the amount of hours you are now expected to dedicate to your job.

A friend of mine was told by a manager that he wasn't putting in a 60 hour week, "The company should be first in your life, and your family second.". The guy came out of the office crying.

An anonymous poster on the less profane vault.com, which refers to itself as the insider career network, has this to say on the "stinking corporate America" message board,

Corporate America is like some private government, mostly unrestrained by countervailing powers of unions, government and civil society. You feel like a slave because workplace democracy is rare at work

For the most part, workers are really working longer hours. Some would even say that their jobs are 24x7 because of the Internet. Pre-Internet days, when I was working for the Securities Industry Automation Corporation (SIAC), all programmers were on call. This meant that if, say at 3 a.m. in the morning, one of your programs bombed out you would most likely be called and asked to trek down to the computer center to fix the problem.

One of my enterprising colleagues was quite fed up with

being called in the middle of the night and so changed his telephone number from his own to Dial-A-Prayer (which I am not sure is still in existence). Of course, my programs were so well-written that I seldom got called (that's a bit of a joke!). But I did get called when they couldn't reach those folks who gave their contact number as Dial-A-Prayer.

It was on a hot hazy night during the summer of 1977 that I got a call such as this. This turned out to be the longest night of my life. It was a rather long, hot night for most of New York as well since on that fateful night the power grid went out - the blackout of 1977 was in full swing.

I worked about 48 hours non-stop during the two days of the power blackout trying to run critical New York Stock Exchange Systems. Merrill Lynch had a center with emergency power just a half mile away, so we lugged hundreds of reels of computer tape down 21 flights of stairs and dragged all of this over to Merrill Lynch for processing.

This 48-hour tour of duty was unusual. Today it's not so unusual for someone to be connected to their place of work during all hours of the day and night. First it was the beeper. This enabled your company to page you wherever you wandered off to. Then it was the mobile phone.

This enabled your boss and clients to talk to you all hours of the day and night - including in your car and on the beach. Although I had been connected to my office using a PC and modem for many years before the Internet, it was really the Internet that added a new dimension to this 24x7 work phenomenon.

The Internet coupled with the office Intranet permits you to work anyplace, anytime. All you need is a PC, a modem (and this can be wireless), and a connection to the web. Few people can just call in sick anymore. If they have a computer at home they can merely sit in their bathrobes with a box of tissues on the desk, and accomplish the same amount of work that they would have if they went to work with that nasty cold.

Need to write a report and send it to a dozen coworkers? Your trusty word processor coupled with a broadcast e-mail will work just fine. There are even web enabled high speed printers if that report needs to be collated, bound and then distributed.

You can even hold meetings and give presentations using web services. I just viewed a demonstration of a complicated PC-based software package. The demo was given using the client's PC. He was in California and I was in New York. So how'd he manage to display his software on my PC's display? Instead of flying all the way to New York he signed up for WebEx's (www.webex.com) real-time business meeting service. WebEx, one of the bright stars of the Internet, has created a service which permits folks to meet right on the web. Thousands of corporations use WebEx to work with their customers, prospects, partners, suppliers and even employees.

According to Stephen S. Roach, an economist often quoted in the New York Times, "The dirty little secret of the Information Age is that an increasingly large slice of work goes on outside the official work hours the government recognizes and employers admit to."

Electronic devices ranging from telephones and fax machines and pagers to cell phones and portable e- mail devices mean employees are connected to the work place 24 hours a day, seven days a week. A study by Pitney Bowes, and conducted by the Institute for the Future, indicated that nearly half the respondents to the study report that work related communication has spread far beyond regular business hours.

There really is no escape.

Actually the Internet does permit one form of escape for employees and that is telecommuting.

About a year ago I convinced my boss to let me telecommute. I was spending almost three hours driving to and from work. At the time, I thought I could be more productive at home away from the hustle and bustle of the office.

Telecommuting has become popular. In 2017, it was reported 3.9 million U.S. employees, or 2.9 percent of the total U.S. workforce, work from home at least half of the time, up from 1.8 million in 2005 (115 percent increase since 2005).

Telecommuting is actual tricky business. Not everyone is cut out for it. Our poster on the vault. com message board soon became a bit disenchanted,

Now working alone most days is driving me crazy, and every time I go to the office I feel like an outsider. Recent hires don't know me all that well, and I don't feel part of the organization.

Telecommuting really does have a lot going for it. It helps save the environment - this is no cliche. If you can save one person from getting in his/her car then that's one point for cleaner air.

It also saves companies money by lessening the office space requirement. There are some companies that designate one cubicle for every five telecommuting employees. Using a carefully planned schedule, each telecommuting employee reserves the cube for one day out of the week. Think how much is saved on telephone, electricity and other expenses. Some companies dispense with offices entirely. Employees work from home, or utilize shared workspaces at WeWork or its competitors.

Probably the most important advantage to telecommuting is that it allows companies to retain the services of valued employees that simply cannot get to work any other way.

I met Lori Gardner a number of years ago when I did some consulting for Unisys, the company she worked for. Lori is one of those ultra-talented workaholics who you love to have on your staff - the work gets done and it's done very well.

At the time, Lori worked for Unisys for fourteen years. For most of that time she was responsible for creating those beautiful marketing materials that tech companies are so famous for. Lori worked hard - usually more than twelve hours a day. Lori was a telecommuter,

It's my back. I can't take the strain of an hour commute each way. Plus I cannot stay up all day from early morning to late at night. I have to take breaks and lie down to get the pressure off my back. I put in a hell of a lot more hours telecommuting than I do when I am at the office. When I'm in the office I just can't wait to get out of there. At home, I keep my computer on all the time. I finish up at around 6:30 p.m. Usually at 8:30 I go over and check to see if there is any interesting or important email. If there is, I'll just sit down and work a couple of extra hours.

Lori connected to Unisys using a combination of the web, e-mail and, on occasion, web conferencing to get her job done. Unlike that anonymous vault.com poster Lori doesn't feel isolated at all,

I am an introvert. This works very well for an introvert. I hate all of that chit chat anyway. This makes it easier for me to get along with people. Now I don't have to deal with all the stuff that just drains the energy out of me.

Of course, there is always a downside. One is that it was hard for her to get promoted since she didn't want to drive to the office. One of her colleagues was told that in order for her to get a promotion to management she'd have to come back to work since it would be impossible to manage employees via the Internet. That colleague shut down her home computer and began to drive to the office five days a week. But she became a manager. Lori would be happy to know that in 2019 plenty of managers work from home.

The Internet provides plenty of tools to make employees productive. Yet these same tools might also spur an astounding lack of productivity. Websense, which is a Web filtering company, finds that the average employee spends 21 hours online each week at work versus only 9.5 hours at home. Another study, by Internet research company Find/SVP, determined that the average employee uses an entire workday each week - 7.7 hours surfing non-work related sites. The Conference Board reported that employees spend 90 minutes each day on non-work related sites.

Sites that lure surfers by offering rewards and/or cash don't help matters much. A growing number of web sites are now paying consumers to visit online advertisements, advertiser web sites and to respond to advertiser's emails.

Of course, given the 60+ hour weeks some of these employees "donate" to their employers a little surf-time is not really a bad thing. So, it's not really the time spent surfing the web that should be an issue here, it's what these employees are actually doing on the web.

Internal Revenue Service Deputy Inspector General Pamela Gardiner looked at how more than 16,000 of the tax collection agency's employees were using their government-owned computers. Of the 16,275 hours the IRS workers spent on the Internet during a seven-day period, 8,250 hours were spent on non-work-related activity ..... Workers were downloading pornography, gambling, shopping online, trading stocks and participating in chat rooms. Departing Senate Finance Committee Chairman Charles Grassley noted that during the most recent tax season, 37 percent of taxpayers calling the IRS for information did not get their calls answered.

Perhaps this isn't such a bad thing after all!

Remember vault.com? It's just one of the many job related

message boards that have popped up on the Internet in recent years. Many of these boards are related to specific companies and current and past employees use them to let the company's dirty laundry wave in the breeze - like this thread about a former senior manager of PriceWaterhouseCoopers who had won a $1.625 million sex discrimination case,

A man who complains about things being unfair gets nothing, someone said. A woman or minority who complains about things being unfair gets what - a well-deserved $1 million and a free ride to partner? Anyone have any example of the stellar work she has done that earned her the position? Another asked, referring to the female partner. She wouldn't know how to fill out a corporate or partnership tax return if her life depended on it.

The numerous message boards only reflect what many people are really thinking, something the media often neglect to consider. The media, unfortunately, is rarely even-handed in their approach to any controversial issue. There are right-leaning (or Republican) publications that are usually against affirmative action, worker rights, etc. Then there are left-leaning (Liberal/Progressive Democrat) publications that are all for affirmative action, workers rights, rain forests, etc. What you will never find in these publications is the other side of the issue. Right is always right. And left is always left. There is no room for debate. The forums, right or wrong from your individual perspective, permit this. But some people really do go too far.

In one example, an employee set up a web site claiming to be another employee and offering to have sex. Sometimes it can get even uglier than this. There have been many cases of e-mail or text stalking - which is when someone sends a continual stream of threatening or pornographic messages. And then there's the case of Dmitry Pruss.

Mr. Pruss was an Russian scientist working at the National Institutes of Health on an exchange scholar visa in the early

1990s when he started using the Internet to take part in online discussions with other expatriates of the former Soviet Union. One day in 1994, an allusion he made to the Holocaust from his government agency account was taken out of context and reposted in a vicious note sent to hundreds of message groups, especially those devoted to discussion of Jewish topics. The attack message against Mr. Pruss read, in part: "As a religious Jew I am OUTRAGED that my tax money is being used to pay for Internet access for the notorious Jew-hating Russian punk". In the next few weeks many of those that read the posting contacted Mr. Pruss' employer and thus began the NIH investigation. Mr. Pruss, a Jew himself, was stunned by the attack. Ultimately he was exonerated, but not before damaging his reputation and future job prospects.

Sometimes being totally "out there" on a message board can work in your favor. This happened to Brock Meeks who wrote a tech column in his spare time that was often opinionated, profane and quite funny. Ultimately MSNBC.com noticed him and hired him on as a technology reporter.

Then there are those folks who have found a great financial use for these message boards proving the old adage that there is a "sucker born every minute" although among those using the Internet you can say that there are ten suckers born every minute.

Washington, DC, December 15, 1999 -- The Securities and Exchange Commission today filed civil fraud charges against three Southern California residents, two of whom are recent UCLA graduates, for manipulating the price of a thinly-traded stock by spreading false information on the Internet message boards, allowing them to reap $364,000 in trading profits.

And of course who can forget the case of the 15 year old wunderkind who used message boards and spam touting stock he had just purchased. He then sold all of these shares, usually within 24 hours, profiting from the increase in price his messages had caused. His profits from each trade ranged from more than $11,000 to nearly $74,000.

This larcenous kid used multiple fictitious author names for the hundreds of identical messages he posted during each manipulation. The postings he made to Internet website message boards included baseless price predictions and other false and/or misleading statements. For example, he claimed in one of his messages that a company trading at $2 per share would be trading at more than $20 per share "very soon." Other postings claimed that a stock would be the "next stock to gain 1,000%," and was the "most undervalued stock ever." The posted messages always caused the price and volume of the touted stocks to increase dramatically.

Internet-related investment problems have become so severe that the Securities and Exchange Commission now conducts annual "International Internet Surf Days". Thirty-eight regulatory authorities dedicate about 300 staff members to surf the Internet for fraudulent solicitation of investors, manipulation, the circulation of false or misleading information and insider trading.

What should concern employers is that some of this "investment spamming" is being done on company time, using a company e-mail address, making the company indirectly responsible for the message - and the financial results of that message.

There are just a lot of folks who are working on their own nowadays. So a natural question is whether the birth of the Internet has either positively or negatively impacted those who choose to go it alone.

It really looked promising in 1995 when the commercial web made its entrance. Shunned, at least initially by big business, the Web looked like Valhalla to most small business people - particularly those that were self-employed. They finally had a marketing venue that was low-cost but had vast potential to connect these small fries to potential clients.

This initial euphoria was short-lived as big business discovered the advantages of being on the Web and as Internet-only companies began to compete with traditional bricks and mortar based businesses. The internet, as it turned out, would be no free ride.

One of the first industries to feel the brunt of this sea change was the travel industry. While large travel agencies such as Liberty Travel, that typically buy airline and hotel space in bulk to offer deep discounts to passengers, are holding their own the independent travel agent is struggling.

A Wilmington North Carolina travel agent says 11 airlines conspired to push her and other colleagues in the state out of business by cutting their commissions.

Sarah Futch Hall, owner of Travel Specialists, filed a class-action lawsuit against the airlines. Ms. Hall said in her lawsuit that the cuts have forced her to increase her fees, thus discouraging clients from dealing with her and encouraging them to buy from airlines on the Internet instead. She accuses the airlines of conspiring to "force all travel agents out of business and usurp that business".

The airlines big push to the Internet might just cost more than travel agents' livelihoods. Orbitz was originally a joint venture between the largest US carriers. Today, it is part of the Expedia umbrella, which also includes Travelocity, hotels.com, and Trivago. At its inception, a study by MIT economics professor Jerry Hausman found that Orbitz would cost consumers $3.2 billion in higher airfares; chill price competition and harm low-cost carriers; and create a "market power ringmaster" which will allow its airline owners to jointly agree in anticompetitive initiatives they could not enforce individually. "We saw the Orbitz venture as the 'Death Star' aimed at destroying once and for all the opportunity of travel agents and other travel retailers to compete on the Internet", said Richard M. Copland, CTC, ASTA president and CEO.

About the only way for the small company to compete against the "big guys" today is to have a forward thinking association going to bat for them. The real estate industry is a good example of this. You may not know this but the National Association of Realtors is a bona-fide dot-com millionaire. But first, a little background.

Back in the good old days there was room in the market for a wide variety of stores and services. Independent pharmacies sat next store to independent travel agencies which, in turn, sat next store to independent bookstores. Then the "big box stores" arrived. Walmart, Kmart and their brethren transformed the way consumers shop - seemingly overnight.

Along with the proliferation of enclosed shopping malls, these big box stores tend to drive business away from the small businesses located either in the town center or in the many strip malls surrounding these towns.

Because they're so large people living close by tend not to like them either as their presence tends to be accompanied by additional traffic, noise and pollution.

"It's doesn't belong there", said Mary McCarty, who has opposed regional big box stores since 1995 ..... Residents wanted a strip mall with a variety of businesses they could use, instead of a company selling milk by the bucket.

Perhaps a letter in response to a column in the New York Times defending chain stores best sums up public sentiment about these stores,

Large Chain stores, with their high staff turnover, can never provide the service of mall local specialty stores. The column ignores the role that small neighborhood stores fill for older shoppers who, using public transportation or traveling on foot, are not likely to be impressed by acres of parking spaces at the mall. Small businesses are, and always have been, the lifeblood of their communities. They support Little League teams, the school plays, the Junior League fund-raisers and so on.

While I occasionally shop at a Big Box I much prefer the non-uniform quirkiness of a small store. It's truly a dull life that's spent in a mall. If you stand in the center of a mall, a Target or a Walmart you can actually lose your sense of where you are - you can be in Kansas, California, New York or on the planet Mars. Dull, indeed!

When the Internet moved into high-gear this Big Box phenomenon moved onto the Web as well and was renamed disintermediation. The term was popularized to describe a prediction that Internet-only companies would effectively eliminate all intermediaries (i.e. travel agents, realtors, booksellers, etc.).

This is what happened to the bookselling business, now a shadow of its independent self.

"Do you have any idea how beleaguered the independent book industry is?" Cass Franks asks. The American Booksellers Association has seen it membership reduced from more than 5,000 to a bit more than 3,000 in just five years. Independent booksellers, like many other independent businesses, have been fighting a seemingly futile battle against international conglomerates like Barnes & Noble, big box chain stores, and Internet-based competitors, such as Amazon. "The entire business is under stress". "Amazon.com changed everything", says Karen Pennington, president of the Northern California Independent Booksellers Association. "Our customers started coming in with printouts, page after page of books we couldn't get. For the first year, we got a bloody nose every time we opened the door".

Amazon.com was at least (initially) a bookseller.

Margaret's a lovely woman who is as talented as she is business savvy. In the antiques business for 25 years, she does it for love as well as for financial reasons. Since the advent of eBay, however, she's had to do it purely for love.

eBay has basically wrecked the antiques business as we know it. Before, people would go into antiques stores and find things that they had never seen before – like rare jewelry. Now they see it on eBay and they figure they can get it anytime, for a lower price. What used to be an appreciation of art is now like a stock market transaction which is driving the value of the objects down.

Margaret goes on to say that more than a few antiques stores have closed as a result and there are fewer worthwhile antiques shows to attend,

What people may be realizing is that when they went to stores and to shows they would socialize. With eBay all of this socialization is gone and there is more isolation - the whole Internet thing has become more isolating.

Margaret is getting out of the business in a few months. Some of her peers, however, are still hanging on and have made tentative forays into using the dreaded eBay.

A lot of dealers back away …. they don't want to be in that society. Some people use eBay just to advertise. They don't actually sell through eBay, instead they use eBay to sell from their own web pages.

eBay is actually a mixed bag. It hurts some and helps others. For some people eBay enables them to hang their shingle where no shingle hung before.

Earning a living online

Colleen Landaiche builds bookshelves. She pays $25 a month to host her website. During her first year, her company brought in $1,000 a month. That's $12,000 a year, folks. Is anyone really making a living going it alone with only the

Internet for company?

I am always amused when a new book or article comes out espousing the brave new world of free agency, or the gig worker. In case you've been on a Safari and out of touch with reality for the past several years free agency is that wonderful myth being perpetrated that, after you've been downsized or just plain booted out the door of your last company you will immediately become a successful solo contractor – i.e. gig worker.

Free agency is not a US-only phenomenon. Great Britain's Department of Trade and Industry published a report remarking on the trend that more and more people are becoming - by choice or circumstance self-employed. One of the commentators on this report, discussing a need for governmental regulation as well as support systems, jokingly states, "As for the minimum wage, I know some self-employed people who would be happy to be able to pay it for themselves".

Interestingly, most of the bestsellers on the topic were written by people who are astonishingly well-connected and need never fear minimum wage or unemployment. Daniel Pink, who authored "Free Agent Nation", was Al Gore's chief speechwriter. Robert Reich, who penned "The Future of Success", was U.S. Secretary of Labor. Their rolodexes will assure them that they will be perennially successful as free agents - never needing to worry whether there's enough money in the till to cover this month's health insurance premiums.

And then there's the matter of retirement. Unless a free agent is successful, retirement might have to be postponed as long as possible. In fact, in this age of downsizing, layoffs and job-hopping employees a comfortable retirement just might be out of the question for most of us.

Some of the companies I worked for did not provide any pensions, and certainly not portable pensions. Unlike the careers of many men in their sixties who have worked for one or two companies all their lives and who were guaranteed a pension, my career was such that job changes and advancements did occur, but not without what is now a long-term penalty. Salaries were always defined (no stock options), and saving was not even a word I could think about until my youngest son graduated from college.. America's philosophy of economic independence certainly does not help some of us even consider the word "retirement".

The truth of the matter is that, as discussed in the early sections of this chapter, employees have become disposable commodities to be hired when times are good and laid off when times are bad. In between workers are left to fend for themselves. But they are given the nice sounding name of free agents once their unemployment runs out.

Of course, there are many of us that truly want to be in business for ourselves and have finely tuned the techniques that Pink and Reich discuss in their respective books as being necessary for success. The majority of independents, however, flail around. And there are many people for whom free agency is simply not an option. I've never heard of a free agent garbage collector or policeman. Nor does everyone have the capacity or even desire to be a free agent.

Many small business owners need to supplement their business income with other sources of income, possibly full-time work. The truth of the matter is that many small businesses just don't generate enough money to pay their own upkeep without considerable outside assistance. This assistance comes in the form of an additional - possibly full-time - job or the income of a spouse.

The Internet has permitted a flood of people to work their businesses part-time. If it pays off they say "great", if it doesn't well, they just won't leave their day jobs just yet.

One hot and heavy area of free-agency is the web

development business. Starting in the mid-1990s Mom and Pop and their nephew Hugey all began to build web sites for the projected hundreds of thousands of businesses that needed to have a presence on the Web. It was great while it lasted. It even provided a nice, fat income for a while. Today, there are fewer independent web designers in the field.

What happened? Other than the fact that literally tens of thousands of people got into the business, the big boys decided that this was too lucrative a revenue stream to pass up. In addition, simple websites can often be generated online via templates for small change.

While independent web developers are most certainly still in business, they are far fewer in numbers and profits. If you're going to be in business on the 'Net it's best to find a niche in which the big boys don't want to compete. Like garlic.

Kevin Broderick grows garlic. Actually, his day job is as an environmental technician at the Sikorsky Aircraft Corporation in Stratford, Connecticut. His next door neighbor is a potter. Together they are going to offer garlic in ceramic pots to web surfers. Katherine WalshBurke is an oncology social worker and full-time professor by day and a bereavement candle maker and Internet shop keeper by night. Andrew Starr argues legal cases in the morning and in the evening he's the webmaster of several "how-to" websites.

The thing that these three have in common is that they're all doing the Net-thing part time. How much do they earn? Starr admits to $5,000 in profits over the years while Walsh-Burke expects to gross about $32,000. They're not quite dot-com millionaires.

When I started my own business I subscribed to a magazine provocatively titled "Midnight Engineering". The editor of this tome, (one Bill Gates and not the one you are thinking of), directed at fully employed hardware and software engineers who wanted to earn a little bit on the side, lived and worked in San Francisco. Sometime during the first year of my subscription I received a mailing from him saying that he was moving out to Colorado. The reasoning was simple. It was too expensive in California and in his new little town of Rocky Ford, Colorado he could buy not only a house to live in but a printing press with which to print his magazine.

The key to business success is to keep expenses low. Bill knew this. Unfortunately, for many reasons, sometimes we are prisoners of our geographic surroundings. In the New York area, where I am from, expenses are astonishingly high. This means that if you want to free agent in New York City you had better be very successful, be gifted with a large inheritance, have a well-paid spouse or take in lots of roommates - this last technique being the technique of choice of the hordes of college graduates that converge upon New York each June.

The Internet does permit us to keep expenses at a minimum. That and the willingness to spend grueling hours "working the 'Net" can bring you a modicum of success, even if that success is not defined in a truckload of dollars.

@EDUCATION

Lee Iacocca

When I graduated from college I decided to take a couple of years before earning any real money and become a teacher. This was back in the early 1970s, a period of time, happily (for me at any rate), coincident with some radical new approaches to teaching.

When I went to elementary school back in the sixties schools and teachers followed a script that went largely unchanged for hundreds of years. Students, all dressed neatly in starched shirts or crinolines, sat in rows of unimpeded evenness with teacher enthroned at the head of the room. Invariably a woman, with a few notable exceptions including my sister's fourth grade teacher Mr. Ferme who was the dreamboat of all the little girls at PS 111 in Queens, New York, Mrs. Teacher was long on discipline and even longer on the three 'Rs - reading, writing and arithmetic (please, someone inform everyone that technically it's really one "R", one "W" and one "A"). I don't remember much creativity but then I really did learn how to read, write and add.

In the seventies, however, learning theory was starting to change. Rote gave way to participatory and regimented was giving way to open. When I took the helm of my own class, "open classroom" was all the rage. In my version of this model, the classroom became a workroom where students were encouraged to work at their own pace on projects of their own choice. Did this work? I'm not really sure. My students were gifted to begin with, coming from good homes in affluent neighborhoods. Some thirty years later I believe that they learned in spite of these open classroom techniques rather than because of these techniques. Since "open classroom" is no longer on the educational radar screen I suspect that the entire concept was thrown in the trash. Over the last thirty years, years that I've not been teaching elementary school, I hazard a guess that dozens more "great ideas" are lying at the bottom of a landfill somewhere.

Education has, and always will be, in a pickle. Let's look at the facts. There is a shortage of folks wanting to become teachers. Given the extraordinarily low rate of pay can you really blame them?

New York City is one of the largest school districts in the United States. Teacher salaries in New York range anywhere between $31,000 and $70,000 with the high end going to those with advanced degrees and years of experience. Oddly, administrative salaries range anywhere between $60,000 and $115,00 - which is quite an interesting dichotomy. Even more astonishing is that as of this writing the school chancellor earns a shameful $352,763!!! New York City is by no means extravagant with their money, except for the bureaucrats it would seem.. On average, a teacher leaving New York for its suburbs can expect an immediate raise upwards of 20 percent -

and far better working conditions.

New York City public schools is typical of urban school districts in this brave new millennium. Hit hard by a mass exodus of retiring and just plain tired teachers, the Board has had to be creative in filling thousands of vacancies - including traveling to often exotic far away places such as Italy to plug these gaping holes.

To compensate for thousands of these novice teachers, the Board of Education has implemented what is being referred to as education by script. Every minute of every hour of every day is scripted for new teachers leading critics to bemoan the lack of creativity and question the results.

The New York City Board of Education has more than just a lack of teacher problem to contend with. A vast majority of its students come from poor families and are quite deficient in both their social and academic skillsets.

Some see the Internet as a panacea for these ills.

Andrew Rasiej is the founder of Civic Hall, a collaborative work center, and event space currently located in the Flatiron district of Manhattan supporting a growing community of people and organizations building technology solutions for the public good. Back in the early 2000s his dream was to wire New York City schools - actually one school in particular. Washington Irving High School is located in the Gramercy Park section of New York City. Gramercy Park is itself quite legendary. A green oasis with lush foliage and the most magnificent of flowers in the Spring, Its wrought iron fence keeps out everyone but the lucky few who happen to hold keys. These lucky folks are the people who live in the elegant townhouses and apartments bounding the park itself. Washington Irving High School is quite near to the park but you can be sure that none of its students live in any of those million dollar homes abutting the park made famous by history and "Time and Again", a turn of the century cult novel by Jack Finney.

Although few people talk about it the hard fact is that nearly 100% of white, affluent children depart the New York City school system (at least in Manhattan) after elementary school. Middle and High Schools are almost entirely composed of minority children. Private schools are de rigueur for affluent white New Yorkers.

While this does not drain city, state or federal funding out of the school system (until, of course, a school voucher system is implemented) it does drain the extra time and money donated by affluent parents. The school system, therefore, really does depend on benefactors such as Rasiej. But Rasiej ran into some unexpected difficulties.

New York City is one of the oldest public school systems in the country. It will come as no surprise that its stock of buildings is some of the oldest in the country as well. Rasiej found this out the hard way. He was trying to give 1,000 Irving students continuous Net access by paying for a T1 connection and having 54 work stations installed in a new Net lab. The school building was not cooperating. At the time it was 85 years old and had asbestos problems. The teachers' union balked at this idea as well. They preferred that the money be spent on fixing several schools rather than on just wiring one school.

The union had a point. And they were not alone. Dr. Doris Sweeney is a teacher in a Central Florida school district as well as a professor at the University of Phoenix Online. She sees a massive schism between types of school districts which affects what that school can expect to accomplish.

As a parent, if you see the need for your school to have a health aide in the clinic, and if the school sends out notices indicating that they need all the parents to chip in five dollars to do this, those parents would chip in the five dollars and it would be done. If you move to another cultural area where you have the same scenario and you ask them to chip in five dollars because the legislature has not funded school nursing or a clinic attendant you are not going to have the same response.

I used to think that the digital divide was a pretense out there but then I started thinking of the experiences I had when I was a high school teacher in an inner city school ..... the school was at the bottom of the list in getting equipment and getting retrofitted. If the teachers didn't write grants it didn't happen. The parents that screamed the loudest got the most. If you walked into classrooms in the 1990's you would expect to see at least one computer in every classroom. But there are still schools in this district! In that have zero to 2 computers in classrooms and it's not because the teachers don't want them. Would you rather spend money putting computers in or buying the reading series so the children can learn to read? It's just a very political issue here. The school I am in is basically a paycheck to paycheck community. With a 55-60% Hispanic population they (the parents) are more interested in helping their children learn English and improve their reading skills than worry about how many computers are in the classroom.

The "digital divide" is very much an in vogue term today. It simply means that there are far too many poor people without access to computers which, many pundits think, will have an extremely adverse affect on their future earning abilities.

Some disagree with this assessment, including former FCC chairman Michael Powell. In fact, he doesn't call it a digital divide at all;

I think there is a Mercedes divide. I'd like to have one; I can't afford one. I'm not meaning to be completely flip about this. I think it's an important issue. But it shouldn't be used to justify the notion of essentially the socialization of the deployment of the infrastructure.

Is there really a digital divide? It's an interesting debate.

Statistics clearly show that there is a wide disparity between the Internet usage rate of minorities versus others. However, in 2013, the Census Bureau reported that 80.9 percent of households below the poverty level had cell phones, and a healthy majority—58.2 percent—had computers. So, clearly the divide is narrowing.

Chairman Powell's lack of enthusiasm for the "socialization of the infrastructure" is quite valid in terms of costs. If the annual cost of a computer and Internet service is about $380 a year, and you were to directly subsidize only 5-10 million of the country's 40-50 million households the cost would be $635 to $1.27 billion a year.

So how do we handle funding? Transfer of wealth from one class of people to another is not always feasible. The American taxpayer, particularly the middle class, is being "nickel and dimed" to death and becoming more and more resentful over the imposition of fees for funding public programs that they can never take advantage of and scholarships and other educational opportunities that they are deemed too wealthy for. They feel that they are working long hours to pay for things like computers and Internet access while, at the same time, the government is taxing them so that others can get it for free. Current democratic presidential candidates Bernie Sanders and Elizabeth Warren's suggestion that we tax the 1% just might be the solution we are looking for.

Middle School 44, located on the Upper West Side in Manhattan, has an interesting approach to raising money for its technology lab. They've been hosting a school-yard flea market and antiques fair for decades. It's a simple formula that can be followed by school districts and/or PTAs everywhere.

The Girl Scouts have been practicing a different soft of self-funding for over one hundred years. Who can ignore a little girl in uniform when she comes knocking at your door - particularly when the cookies she's selling are chocolate covered mints.

South Dakota is large on land but small on population. The Governor was concerned about his multiple school districts with fewer than 600 students. Many of these schools could only provide a basic curriculum giving new meaning to the term digital divide. The Governor, however, was committed to equalizing education by using the Internet. Unfortunately, the cost to wire 622 buildings so that three out of four students could simultaneously use the Internet was about $100 million.

The Governor needed to be creative. And he was. He commissioned 11 teams of inmates from the South Dakota corrections system and had them trained to install 101,250 commercial grade network connections. The state provided supervisors and materials and the schools provide food and lodging. The Governor used state and federal education improvement funding to provide the $15 million needed to connect the classrooms while the local school boards, with the help of local businesses, paid for the computers.

All that you need is a bit of motivation.

As I've already stressed, it's getting hard to find qualified teachers. Actually, it's getting hard to find any teachers; thus the wholesale importation by some communities of untrained retirees, ex- business people and language and American-culture deprived foreign teachers.

At the same time that we are suffering a crisis in finding and retaining good teachers we are also seeing our costs per student escalating dramatically. It doesn't take a great mathematical mind to project that there is a vast shortfall between the amount of money collected via the typical real estate tax funding method and the amount of money expended.

In future we can expect to need ever-increasing amounts of money. The population has grown somewhere around 13.2%. A large proportion of this increase is due to immigration. Given this trend, it has been projected that, sometime after the year 2050, America's population will be more than 50% minority.

An increasing minority population presents some interesting problems. According to the 2000 census while an average 34% of whites and 53.9% of Asian/Pacific Islanders in the 25 through 29 age category have a Bachelor's degree or higher, only 17.8% of (non-Hispanic) Blacks and 9.7% of Hispanics can claim the same level of educational attainment. Similarly, 94% of whites and 93.5% of Asians in this same age category have completed High School with Blacks and Hispanics lagging behind with 86.8% and 62.8% respectively.

Census Bureau data indicate that Hispanics in the United States are growing poorer. Between 1989 and 1998, annual income for Hispanics dropped 14%, from approximately $26,000 to less than $22,900. Hispanics now make up almost 24% of the poor in this country. Hispanics are experiencing a downward economic slide. Even the increasing number of illegal Hispanic immigrants in the country, who tend to have little education, lack English-language skills, and hold service sector jobs, have not distorted these results. A number of researchers believe that lack of education is responsible for the downward trend..

So, in the America of 2050, we have an increasingly undereducated population whose poverty precludes the increases in property taxes that will need to make its way into future school budgets, not to mention the people power that will be required to run an increasingly knowledge intensive labor market, particularly if the trend of "tossing out" older workers continues. If these extrapolations are accurate it appears that America could very well become a third world country.

Nearly 20% of the original class of 2000 [New York City] dropped out. Only 50% of city students complete high school in four years, 60% of elementary and middle school pupils can't read at grade level and 70% are not proficient at math. At Community School

66 in the South Bronx, nearly 80% of the pupils in grade 4 failed at reading. A few days ago, I was speaking to Paul Vallas who just quit as head of Chicago's public schools .... He had just given a commencement address at an elementary school where 40% of the students live in foster care and 90% come from homes where two parents were not present. All the kids were poor ..... A whole bunch of people have dropped their duty and thrown in the towel .... The list of criminals would include a ton of bureaucrats at City Hall, the mayor right up top, school administrators, a lot of politicians, an entire parade of parents ....

This is not a book of answers. But it is a book about possibilities. The Internet is one such possibility.

Since the future will find us short on money and teachers but long on challenges, the Internet just might be an important part of a solution to this most complicated problem. Certainly, the middle and more affluent classes have latched onto the concept in a variety of ways. One of these ways is as an adjunct to homeschooling.

Mary Higgins is my favorite 17 year old and I don't even know her. I met her through an e-mail when she responded to a "call for papers" that I broadcast over the Internet for a book I was editing on Internet development techniques. She wrote a chapter for me that was well written and concise. When I found out that she was a home schooled high-schooler I could only e-mail kudos to her parents.

I use the Internet for research, ideas, and sometimes help. You can find more information on the web than at your local library. Especially since my library is very small. It is in an old house with about three rooms of books. Kind of hard to find much on a certain topic I might be looking for.

I've found that being home schooled has brought my grades up. In public school I received A's and B's now I mostly receive A's or B+'s. when you don't have to fight 30 other students for attention from the teacher you can learn more. I can take things at my own pace and if I don't understand something I can work it out until I do.

I do have normal school books just like any other school. My class is a computer program, which is linked to the Internet and is helpful during essays. You can, though, take complete high school lessons over the Internet, and college. I don't know how or if those work, but I would still rather go to a real college or public school. I don't like home schooling that much anymore. It's getting boring and I think because I'm not challenged anymore.

I use the net to chat a lot with friends. I can express myself better online, because I'm very shy in person, and I don't have to worry because they can't see me at that moment. I will say that you can become addicted to the Internet, I was and maybe still am a little, but since I have gotten more friends I have spent more time online. Being home schooled is very lonely at times. I miss having as many friends as I did and getting out of the house a lot more

The Internet can be my escape sometimes from my problems. I can go chat with friends, work on my web site or read a book online. You can meet and talk to a lot of different people online, some even from different countries, but you don't want to get so involved online that you miss out on the things that are going on around you at home. You can't ignore your family so you can talk to someone in England. I used to go in chat rooms but I've stopped because I see too many parents online and ignoring their children. That is why now I've cut back on my online time so I don't grow up to be like that and if I have kids I don't want them online constantly either. There is a life outside of the Internet.

From Mary's perspective home schooling is a mixed bag. It's clear that, at 17, she's ready for the socialization of college. For younger children and their parents, however, the bloom is still very much on the rose. According to the National Home Education Research Institute there are 2.3 million homeschooled children in the United States with this number growing year by year.

Adrienne is a busy beaver at school. She's answered at least 50 questions on Greek mythology and has illustrated the myth of Sisyphus. Although it's past her bedtime she logs on one more time to find that her arch-rival is outwitting her once again. Adrienne is home-schooled - but home-schooled with a difference. She uses the Internet every step of the way. Once she's under the covers she turns on her PowerBook and starts to work on an ode to the Greek god Hephaestus. She doesn't have to wait until the library is open. Using her web browser she has access to all the world's libraries even in the middle of the night.

The Internet has most definitely put Adrienne on par with her school-bound peers in terms of research, a growing collection of interactive online courses and even virtual socialization.

Opponents of homeschooling usually cite this last item, socialization, as a reason why children should attend school. However, several factors cast a shadow over this particular line of reasoning. Eric Harris and Dylan Klebold brought new meaning to the term school socialization. These were the young men responsible for the Columbine school massacre. Unfortunately, this was not an isolated incident. In fact, incidents of violence in US schools are increasing rather than decreasing. In Texas, for example, four 8th grade boys were arrested for conspiracy to commit murder, conspiracy to commit arson, and conspiracy to manufacture explosives after teachers and students overheard conversations about a planned attack on the school.

Ohio University did a study that found that early warning signs of violence are often overlooked by both teachers, school administrators and parents. Richard Hazler, professor of counseling education at Ohio University asked, "when are children just playing and when should an adult intervene?" Hazler studied 251 teachers and counselors in Ohio to assess their understanding of bullying and non-bullying behaviors.

Study participants were given 21 scenarios of different emotional and physical confrontations between kids and asked to identify which were bullying situations. Hazler found that between 50 and 80 percent of the participants, depending on the individual scenario, labeled non-bullying situations as bullying which suggests that professionals are not clear about which situations they should react to and how they should react. Hazler explains,

People are less likely to show concern, attempt to prevent or act to intervene in situations involving potential social or verbal harm while they are more likely to overreact in situations involving potential physical harm. This appears to be just the type of mistake that allowed the young gunmen in recent school shootings, or many youth who attempt suicide who have their own struggles with peer harassment, to go under-attended for months or years. If people aren't recognizing emotional abuse as bullying, these things build up within children and can lead to an explosion or violence as a means of being heard or retaliation in what feels to them like a hopeless situation. What really counts is what goes on inside of a person and from a child's eyes, continuing emotional and social abuse by peers are the most damaging.

School violence and bullying are greatly exacerbated by the massively large schools in which most high school students are warehoused. In this impersonal environment, high numbers of students are paired with overworked and too few teachers. The school day usually begins early and ends early leaving adolescent children two few options for spending their time before the end of the school day and dinner time.

After school activities are also a contributing factor. Many school systems emphasize sports to the detriment of academic study. Jocks are lauded, nerds laughed at and all others are just ignored - or worse. It's not only the students that behave in this manner. Parents and teachers do as well.

Parents, in fact, are a chief cause of a variety of problems for school-age children. In many instances it has been reported, in the aftermath of Columbine-like massacres, that parents were largely uninvolved with their children. In fact, the Columbine killers reputedly stored their cache of weapons right under the noses of one of the parents. Dr. Sweeney, our veteran of the Orlando school system, has even found cases where parents would rather spend their discretionary income on new hairdos or exotic manicures then for the betterment of their own children. It's a matter of parent choices, she says.

Interestingly most proposals to make schools more accountable for the success of its students never take into account that a child's ultimate success or failure truly rests with his or her parents.

In 1996 then President Bill Clinton instituted the Technology Literacy Challenge. Its goal was to increase schools' Internet access and it has to the tune of $2 billion dollars - except in the poorest regions of the country. Here, school districts have untrained teachers, outdated software and unwired or no computers at all. Much of this money comes from the disputed E-Rate program, often dubbed the Gore tax. 19 U.S. senators and representatives signed a letter stating that the FCC's reckless implementation of this program could ultimately cause chaos for our nation's schools and libraries.

In 1999, Kanawha City Elementary School in Charleston, West Virginia was one of 240 schools nationwide to receive the Department of Education's Blue Ribbon award for educational excellence. It won because of its innovative use of technology to nurture critical thinking.

In the computer lab at Kanawha City Elementary School children are huddled over assorted computers searching the Internet for information about shrimp, giant water bugs and mealworms. Jared hits the jackpot by using Ask Jeeves for Kids. His friend Jerry is perusing a Yahoologans-recommended site. What's wrong here? There's not a teacher to be found. Instead these students aren't waiting for anyone to tell them what to do. They're sharing information they've uncovered, comparing search strategies and taking tons of notes. Once they've exhausted all avenues of research they'll start organizing their research, evaluating results and then designing a web site for their completed report. They're practicing independent learning - and exercising their critical thinking skillsets to boot.

But few schools seem to be able to emulate Kanawha City Elementary School in spite of Clinton's massive infusion of money and additional funding from school bonds. Aside from funding, equipment and wiring problems there is another problem that is stalling the migration to web-based education - curricula. Online teaching is quite different from in-person teaching. You can't just toss up a lesson plan online.

Cynthia Thomas is a fourth grade teacher at the Oak Hill Elementary School in Austin, Texas. Her solution to the curricula problem was to turn to Foster City, California based Classroom Connect. Classroom Connect sent Thomas' class on a six week cybertrek across Kenya and Tanzania. What Thomas' class, and scores of others classes in the U.S., got was the daily postings and photos made by Classroom Connect employees and several scientists some 9000 miles away. Uploaded via a laptop and satellite phone, students learned about the countries' history, wildlife and geography. They also got to interact with the team all along the way via e-mail. 11 year old Janelle Revord was so excited about learning all about the Masai tribe that on weekends she started going to the public library to spend even more time on the Classroom Connect web site. "It's not like Texas", says Janelle, "they eat raw goat and drink blood. It was kind of gross".

The educational market is big business. In the United States alone we spend $4 billion on textbooks and instructional technology content. Even the government has gotten involved. The U.S. Department of Education sponsors the Gateway to

Educational Materials which contains more than 14,000 lesson ideas and learning resources from over 200 organizations.

But the online content market is extremely fragmented. A math course for a fourth grade class is different from one for a third grade class. Essentially, thousands upon thousands of courses would be needed to satisfy all ages, grades and subject matters making profitable development of content all but impossible for most private companies. The answer can only come from wholesale government funding of public programs to coordinate the development of these courses by either the school districts or other academic institutions on behalf of the school districts. There is no lack of creativity on the part of educators when properly funded.

Migrant workers often live in ramshackle housing and work from sunup to sunset. They travel across the US from crop to crop. What you might not know is that they usually take their children with them. Far from their friends and fellow students just how do these students keep up with their schoolwork? Up until now they just didn't which often meant that a new generation of uneducated workers was just ripe for the picking. Because of a program funded primarily by the U. S. Department of Education's Office of Migrant Education, a group of Eagle Pass, Texas high school students, far from home, will be graduating from high school on time.

ESTRELLA, which stands for Encourage Students Through Technology to Reach High Expectation in Learning, Lifeskills and Achievement, unites the power of the Internet, the hard work of students and their parents, and a bunch of dedicated educators. Using a laptop computer students must dedicate at least 7 hours a week to their studies· which is not an easy task after spending hours on their knees picking beans. An Internet connection and email account enable students to communicate with teachers, mentors, and friends. The computer benefits more than just the student. Parents also use it to get a better grasp on English and younger siblings benefit by being exposed to technology early on.

In a remote village of South Africa, an abandoned cargo ship container doubles as an Internet cafe for students enrolled in an online-learning program of the University of South Africa. Although the computers are powered by noisy gas-fired electric generators the cafe, funded by the World Bank, allows students to take business and health care courses from professors in Pretoria, some 300 miles away.

Jong Sang-won is studying for his college entrance exam. Last year Jong spent his summer dragging a heavy backpack through downtown Seoul Korea to take classes which would help him get into a prestigious university. It was a sweltering summer, the streets were crowded and the lecture halls were even worse. This year all Jong needs is his laptop. He has been attending an online school that offers lectures in math and physics.

AT&T offers a variety of support for its many thousands of employees who participate in the company's tuition assistance program. More than a few of these employees are now pursuing degrees via web-based programs from institutions such as University of Phoenix Online..

Browne & Co. is a 225 year old financial printer and SEC filing service provider with at least 1,000 globally distributed employees. When they needed to teach their employees some technical jargon it was impractical to have them come back home and take a land-based course. Instead, Bowne & Co. sent their employees to school on the Web.

Vicky Phillips, CEO of distance-learning consultancy geteducated.com, says that online learning isn't for everybody. For it to work students must be extremely motivated to login and do their work. Because it is a computer intensive environment, students have to acclimate to frequent computer and network related problems. Phillips says that these problems, coupled with the loneliness factor, leads to a dropout rate as high as 50 percent.

I started teaching at Fairleigh Dickinson in 1999. The majority of my students were, and continue to be, foreign, hailing from either China or India. Interestingly, this is not just a FDU phenomenon. According to the National Science Foundation foreigners are driving up enrollment in science and engineering programs.

For the most part these students are 20-somethings who want to go to school in person. They enjoy the fraternity of campus life and all the socialization opportunities that being on campus affords.

Late in 2001 I also started teaching, or facilitating as they call it, for the University of Phoenix Online. These students, for the most part, were not quite 20-somethings. They were gainfully employed and, to them, the benefits of UOP meant that they could actually get themselves a degree without quitting their jobs.

Today's workers work longer and harder than ever before - no 9 to 5 here. Traditional schools, particularly in cases where employees have hefty travel schedules, are really out of the question for most modern workers. Statistics bear me out on this. Arthur Levine, former President of Teachers College at Columbia says that the "new online schools are catering to the new American college student". He says that only 16% of the college population is actually on campus. The rest are working people.

Dianne V'Marie is a long time UOP facilitator with an interesting tale to tell.

It had been a rather quiet day until the phone rang. After I spoke with him, everything turned upside-down and I could feel all of those sad, mixed-up emotions we work so hard to keep way down deep inside us come brimming to the surface. His daughter had been in an accident and he was calling me from Intensive Care - couldn't talk long, he wasn't sure she'd make it - and I heard his voice break.

Now some would tell me that I didn't even know the man who called. If you showed me his photograph, it would have been the first time I knew what he looked like - and in fact, I'd never heard his voice before and had he not identified himself, I wouldn't have been even able to guess who he was. Even still, I felt as though I knew this man. Some people think that you must know a person face-to-face to really know someone - I would disagree. This gentleman was one of my Online students and we were going into the fourth week of class. We'd been together five days out of seven, four weeks in a row. The class was an interpersonal communications course - one of my favorites - and in class, we had all spoken about topics that really mattered to us. I knew how much this daughter meant to him. I knew that they had gone through a very rough time with her when she was in her early teens, but somehow, once she'd gotten her driver's license and had more independence - ironically enough - she and her dad had created new bonds and moved into a much more interdependent relationship, much to his deep relief and joy. They had gone on long drives as she struggled to learn how to operate the car - they had changed the oil in the family car together - they had washed and waxed the car at the end of the day. Now that same car was just as crumpled as was the girl.

How could it be that this man's story disturbed me so greatly when I didn't even know how old he was, whether or not he was bald or spectacled, short or tall. By being in a virtual classroom, we don't have many of those barriers that you and I have created right here. I can see you and you can see me - and without my even saying a word to you, you'd already perhaps decided on some things about me, trusting your senses to divine the truth. Online, we base the truths we learn about each other on words - on words and how they are woven. We have few distractions as we ponder various truths and concepts related to the subject matter of the class. We thoroughly delve into the course, twisting and turning significant topics, attempting to approach them from every angle. As a result of that, we get to know the subject - and the people.

If you had told me several years ago that this was the way things happened in an Online class, I would have balked. How could that be? How could you personalize a faceless class? Some four or five years ago, my father took the intensive training to become a UOP Online instructor - as you might imagine, I bombarded him with questions laced with skepticism and doubt about online education. I had been a classroom instructor at the UOP Tucson campus for several years - but how could all of what went on in class there take place on a screen? My dad described how faculty members would start the Online week with a lecture, discussing the various topics covered in the textbook, highlighting the course objectives for that week. He explained to me that he would then design discussion questions that would encourage his students to apply what they had learned in their readings - to link the textbook lessons with things they had observed - and by doing so, every student became a classroom teacher. I asked my dad what his role was, and he went on to tell me that he facilitated the learning by piggybacking on these topics, furthering the discussion, asking questions so the students would dig more.

Surprisingly, my father's explanation paralleled the UOP model I'd applied quite successfully over the years - UOP onground instructors were charged with facilitating the learning - we weren't the talking heads I'd been asked to be with contracts from other universities. UOP didn't want me to hand over the proverbial fish dinner on a platter; my job was to rig up my own gear, and with a flick of an experienced wrist land the lure in just the right place, reel in a glittering, thrashing fish. That wasn't all. Then I was to watch as my observers did the same, guiding them with gentle comments about their gear, about their flick, about their lure, about their fish - what student would be content with the fish I'd caught when so much of the reward of the sport was in the pursuit. Knowing first-hand the thrill of the sport on ground, I quickly became eager to try some of this online fishing.

And so it was that I ventured into my first online classroom - I'd gone through rigorous faculty training where we were taught how to conduct a class successfully, emphasizing the importance of how we "said" things on that screen.

So somehow by participating in our Online classes, we've seen that learning does indeed take place without the traditional sight and hearing processes - we all came to class without the inconvenience of having to go to a physical classroom. In fact, both students and faculty can come to class when we wish, whether it be first thing in the morning or last thing at night or somewhere in-between. And as a bonus, it does indeed appear that human interaction in these classes without walls is still alive and well. In fact, by using a seemingly non-human learning process, we not only learn the material, but I do believe we learn how to become better human beings.

Speaking of that - remember that I began this with my student's tale about his daughter, the one who lost control of her car. Long after the class was over, I got a note. When I saw his name on the list of messages waiting for me to read, I worried - all I needed to do was open that emailed note to discover which road the girl had taken. I wasn't disappointed. It had taken several operations and months of therapy, but she was getting around and had even been able to graduate with her class. It had been a rather quiet day until I opened that message, and I realized then that becoming an Online instructor had enriched my life in ways I'd never have been able to imagine.

When I started to work for UOP I had my own doubts about online degree programs. I didn't think they were rigorous enough. I had already done some course development and online teaching for what is referred to as eduCommerce companies. These companies are in the business of developing courses for free dissemination to the general public. Buyers of these services, such as Dell and Barnes and Nobles, use them as a loss leader to get folks to their respective web sites and buy something (more about eduCommerce later). From this experience I didn't have really high expectations about the quality of either the curricula or the student body.

UOP courses are short. While a usual college semester is about 15 weeks long, an UOP course is between five and eight weeks long. Students typically take one, but rarely ever more than two, courses at a time. If you do the math then you'll find that an UOP student can actually take the same number of credits as a student in a traditional school during the course of a year but is afforded far more flexibility. If a student is expecting to go on vacation or is gearing up for a long business trip then she merely signs up for the next block of courses. So, instead of missing an entire 15-week semester she misses out on, at most, one course.

I first got involved with UOP when they sent me an e-mail in the Fall of 2000 asking me if I wished to teach at UOP. How they got my name, I'll never know. Perhaps it was because I was already facilitating some online EduCommerce courses. Or it may have been because of my tenure at FDU. Who really knows? Anyway, they did solicit me and I, intrigued by the offer, immediately shot back a "yes, I'm interested."

What followed was some nine months of waiting, interspersed with four weeks of training (unpaid) and a five-week mentorship (thankfully, paid). Training consisted of a two week workshop, where we learned the art and science of facilitating an online class and such esoteric skills as how to handle students who don't participate, students who participate too much, students who post angry and/or sexist messages, etc.

While everyone in the training group had degrees up the kazoo, I was disappointed that there was only one other techno-geek (or even business geek) in the group. Instead my particular group, which was one of several being conducted simultaneously, was composed of elementary school teachers, psychologists and others involved in the more "humane" professions. Needless to say that when you start getting into side discussions such as "what colors you are" (and I don't mean whether you're Black or White), you know you've stepped outside of the realm of the scientific.

The two weeks of training was immediately followed by two weeks of observation. This was truly an eye-opening experience for me. Instead of sloppy teaching and ill-prepared students I found the facilitator, Albert Salinas, to be hard-working and ever-present in the online classroom offering thought-provoking questions and good advice. Instead of "hiding in back of the class" each student brought his or her own work-related experience to the mix making this class interesting - even for the non-participating observer.

Online Universities are many and varied but UOP was one of the first. Founded in 1976, the University of Phoenix had at its peak over 500,000 students online and on its various campuses. Once a publicly traded company, with stock soaring to stratospheric heights, it was acquired and is now a non-public organization. Not without its controversies, and the defendant in more than a few lawsuits, and earning the ire of the US Department of Education under the Obama administration, UOP continues to educate its target market of working adults.

While my online class at Fairleigh Dickinson University used a web interface - complete with virtual blackboard – my first class at UOP used Microsoft's Outlook Express which is probably familiar to you as an e-mail program. While Outlook Express was indeed an e-mail program it also handled something called newsgroups (sometimes called discussion groups). In UOP parlance a newsgroup was created for each course. This was the classroom. Within each classroom (i.e. news group) there were several folders. One was for course materials, one for the main discussion area and several more for independent study group usage. Nowadays, UOP, and many others, use state of the art technology such as Blackboard Ultra.

For the most part, teaching is not done during real time. Lectures, assignments and all discussions are mostly handled using asynchronous messaging. This means that the facilitator posts a lecture, video or printed, at, say, 10 a.m. EST and a student can read it at 4 p.m. CST. The beauty of this is obvious. Teachers can teach when they have the time and students can learn when they have the time.

Demands on the student are actually quite rigorous. They can't quite come in, sit in back of the class and take a snooze. Students must actively participate in five out of seven online days during the class week which runs from Tuesday through Monday to take advantage of the weekend.

They can't glide through the courseware either. Each week has the students reading a lengthy section of the text, reading a facilitator-written (or videotaped) lecture, answering several discussion questions - or DQ's as they have come to be known - writing a weekly paper, participating in a study group and ultimately summarizing their week's experiences in a weekly summary.

The students are graded weekly as well. The facilitator uses the online grading module at the end of each week detailing how many points they have earned that week and offering up praise as well as criticism.

Without being a full-time employee this model of online education wouldn't work very well. Because they are full time employees they, with exceptions of course, bring the discipline, writing abilities, and real-world experience that makes taking and teaching these courses worthwhile.

When I first started facilitating for UOP I was already teaching a graduate course for FDU (in person). Upon describing all of the work that UOP students had to do in five weeks all my FDU students could offer up was loud groan. Keep in mind that full time students are masters of trying to get out of work. I've been offered eloquent rationalizations for why term papers aren't needed and why midterms and finals are a waste of time.

While UOP might have been one of the first they certainly aren't one of the last. Most universities are jumping onto the cyber bandwagon.

All this online schooling seems a good idea, doesn't it? There are some interesting caveats to all this good cheer. One of the first things to think about is a lack of choice. Obviously, the vast majority of American students will not be able to cough up the change to enroll at Fuqua. They'll have to look elsewhere. Since most workers are covered by some sort of tuition reimbursement they might well find themselves gently steered to a program that they might not be too keen on. For example, AT&T in Somerset, N.J., at one time actively encouraged all students to register in online programs at either UOP or Thomas Edison State because they forged a deal with these institutions for lower tuition rates and to accept the company's internal classes for credit. Cyber-degrees, already suspect in some people's eyes, moves into an even grayer area of legitimacy once you start co-mingling non-accredited workplace-led instruction with courseware from accredited institutions.

The multi-tier fee structure should also be of concern. If corporate universities unite, they can negotiate prices with today's earnings-driven schools. Corporate Universities, some believe, were founded to end higher education's monopoly on passports to opportunity. Perhaps now is the time to test this assertion. Knowledge is now the central resource of the knowledge economy. Universities and colleges as producers and distributors of knowledge must be challenged. The Corporate University Consortium now under discussion could evaluate various online degree-granting programs, rank them on the basis of important criteria and buy "in bulk" via an Internet-based program "seats on the school bench" for employees.

Where have we heard this argument before? Oh, yes - health care. Today small businesses and individuals not working for a major corporation are often confronted with excessively high health care premiums. As a small business in the state of New Jersey I am paying more for my staff than, say, AT&T. AT&T's negotiating abilities with larger insurers may have driven their employee premium costs down but the health care industry has to get their money from somewhere. That somewhere is my pocket. In essence, I am subsidizing AT&T employees (at least I feel like I am).

Won't the same thing happen in education? As large corporations negotiate ever lower costs from cyber (and even land-based) universities, universities are being put in the position of scrambling for the dollars to meet their ever-increasing costs. Simply put, they have to get their cash from someplace. And this place is probably going to be from an unaffiliated student or a student that works for a small company that is unable to negotiable substantial discounts. Ultimately, will this create a have and have not divide .... and will a quality education be only for the elite? Far from democratizing education, many critics argue, online learning could facilitate the rise of a two-tiered educational system - prestigious campus-based diplomas for the education of the elites, mass-marketed online degrees for those less fortunate.

Another possible bleak future scenario might be the de-professionalization of the university teaching profession. You may have noticed that UOP refers to its staff as facilitators rather than professors.

It's inefficient to have thousands of highly trained, reasonably well-paid professors teaching the exact same courses to students around the country. Why not take advantage of the Internet's ubiquity ... to deliver courses online, educating thousands or millions of students at a time instead of a mere dozens or hundreds. Education scholars William Massy and Robert Zemsky argue that universities must use technology to trim teaching expenditures. With labor accounting for 70 percent or more of current operating cost, they assert, there is simply no other way.

Some even predict a day when star professors at Harvard and elsewhere would become free agents similar to professional athletes, able to sell their services to online ventures and their student "customers."

Carol Geary Schneider, President of the Association of American Colleges and Universities based in Washington D.C., also worries that cyber-schools will cannibalize traditional schools,

All of these programs, even when they are done very well, ultimately are parasitic on established universities. Most of the early programs that served adult learners relied on faculty who held full time appointments somewhere else. There has been an unexamined assumption that somewhere we are investing in the intellectual development of this faculty and that alternative providers can draw on the shared knowledge base and community of scholars and intellectual work that has been the foundation of the university in the 20th century.

Cyber-universities are now assuming, in fact, that they can continue to find qualified faculty on a mass scale to come in and be adjuncts from anywhere and everywhere. But their quality depends on our quality and if you drain the quality of our core institutions everyone will lose. We may find ourselves going the way of many public schools, with thinly trained people often doing a very unsatisfactory job.

Schneider is even more concerned about the nature of

learning in some of the virtual universities,

My particular concern is the notion of the canned course that is scripted by professor so and so, who is nicely paid for her work, after which professor so-and-so goes away, the course goes in a catalog and there's a plan for how to teach it. People who never met professor so-and-so will then be hired to teach this course and the student is supposed to take up to 40 such courses from all over the country or the world and call the result a university education.

There is a problem with the notion of an education that is assembled from bits and pieces from anywhere and everywhere, designed in virtual cyberspace by faculty who had no connection with each other and no connection with the students. It's a crazy-quilt approach that violates every known principle for fostering powerful learning in students.

I am not saying that it [cyber-education] cannot be done well. I am saying that none of the principles for excellence developed by pioneering programs [for non-traditional Learners] are being applied in many of these new designs for distance and distributed learning.

American Federation of Teachers former President Sandra Feldman concurs with this view. "Clearly the growing popularity of distance education calls for a close look at its application and an emphasis on developing and maintaining high standards. While online and distance learning are in general good options for taking a particular course or set of courses, this does not automatically mean that it is acceptable for an entire undergraduate degree program to have no in-class component."

Ultimately the market will make the decision as to the ultimate success or failure of these virtual universities. If students graduating from these schools perceive themselves to be losing out on job opportunities to campus-based graduates the mad rush to cyber-schooling will slow and the virtual university will need to be rethought and possibly reinvented.

Several years ago I was invited to write two courses for a new start-up eduCommerce company called notHarvard. eduCommerce, a term purportedly coined by the folks at notHarvard. notHarvard was quickly renamed Powered as a result of a threatened lawsuit by the real Harvard University and is now defunct. The company provided free mini-courses as a hook to generate site visits. Dell computer used this technique as did Barnes and Noble and a wide variety of other institutions.

Courses typically contained eight or so lessons, homeworks and quizzes which are posted to the client's web site (e.g. Barnes and Noble) once or twice a week. Students interacted with each other and the course facilitator using a message board.

Now I've both written these courses as well as facilitated them and I will say there are many major shortcomings to this variety of e-education. First, the courses are simply too short to cover anything in substantive detail. That's probably why the bulk of these courses are light topics such as "Jazz: A History of America's Music" and "Eyewitness: America Through the Eyes of Its Photographers."

Offering more technical or knowledge-intensive courses has its problems in addition to shortness of the courses and the message board mode of instruction. Class registrations for popular courses can in the thousands - a number way too high for any personalized instruction – as the less than stellar success of most modern-day MOOCs (Massive Open Online Course) will attest. In addition, many of the students who take these free online courses are often woefully unprepared for the topic.

One of the courses I penned for Powered was called "Introduction to Visual Basic". The course clearly stated its pre-requisites which included some programming experience and a copy of the software. It utterly amazed me that dozens of students had signed up for the class without either of these prerequisites. My question? How can you learn a programming language if you don't have the programming tool?

I also found that many of these students were not patient enough to learn a difficult topic online. They gave up far too quickly. If they couldn't figure out the answer in just a few minutes they immediately posted a question to the message board, regardless if that question was already posted - and answered - elsewhere on the board. Although, in fairness to these students, I will say that a web-based discussion board, is a rather cumbersome way to learn. It's also difficult to control. Learning a programming language requires patience and a lot of trial and error.

When I teach non-virtual students how to program I make them spend considerable amounts of time in exploring solutions to a programming exercise. In a virtual classroom, with an uncontrolled message board, you'll always have a student quick to give up and ask for the answer. You also always have the equivalent of the class show-off who immediately raises his or her hand to provide the answer - without allowing anyone else to figure out the answer for themselves. I don't know why they do it, but every introductory course I've ever taught has had one or more experts sign up just to "show off" their advanced skillsets. The problem here is that providing students with immediate answers means that they'll never learn how to do it for themselves.

While Arthur Levine, former president of Teachers College at Columbia University predicts that, within 10 or 15 years, we might just have holograms of a student's professor and fellow students generated right from his or her PC, right now the Powered web-based interface is more the norm.

"Sure you can get (expletive) free from a vending machine .... soak a dollar bill in salt water and put it in the machine. Then ..

push any of the buttons, as many times as you want," one student said in a message to the Google group alt.phreaking while another student turned to the Internet for help with an extracurricular chemistry project making illegal drugs.

This was all done on school time and with school equipment leading one to ask the question "just who is monitoring these kids?"

Interestingly, one of the problems with virtual education might be its biggest selling point - the kids have to participate - and it just might be too much work for some of them. Students cannot sit in the back of a classroom and daydream in the online environment. They must participate in a discussion, respond to a question, engage in a chat room, or submit an assignment to be counted as present. In a traditional class, if a student just shows up, passes tests and hands in assignments on time she passes the course with flying colors. All of this prompted one straight-A student to drop out of online classes stating that the courses were much more work than he was accustomed to.

Advantages to online education far outweigh any perceived disadvantages. Virtual schooling is far more inclusive than traditional schooling barring neither the physically, mentally handicapped or child with the occasional bout of acne severe enough to keep him or her home from school. As you've seen, homeschoolers will never be at a disadvantage and the children of migrant workers can get their high school diplomas on time. The horizons of all ages of students are expanded. Virtual tours of foreign lands and distant times can only enhance traditional models of learning.

For the older worker virtual schooling also offers the advantage of getting re-trained from the comfort of their homes. When LTV Mine shut down workers were offered grants to attend virtual Capella University and be retrained in other fields.

THAT'S
@ENTERTAINMENT

Andrew Tyler likes buying things on eBay. In fact, in a short period of time, Tyler bid on and won over $925,000 (you read that right) worth of merchandise including a 1955 Ford convertible, a Van Gogh painting and a 1971 red Corvette. Trouble is that Tyler's an eighth-grader and he probably has no more than $25 to his name. He thought eBay was a game! The Internet sure is fun.

Last week I surfed over to Netflix and watched a few minutes of a full length movie on my PC. Actually it was going to be for just a few minutes so I could tell you what it was like, but that few minutes turned into an hour and forty as I sat transfixed by "Final Approach". The movie is about an Air Force stealth pilot who has an accident and wakes up with a face he doesn't recognize and in a place he'd never been before. Netflix isn't alone in offering tons of movies, documentaries. There's Hulu, Amazon Prime Movies, YouTube and the list goes on and on and on.

A few decades ago Napster, a young start-up, came up with a way to enable people to download music (illegally) on demand.

The music industry vigorously defended their copyrights and actually won one for the gipper, but the handwriting was already on the wall. Some people just want to download their entertainment.

During the summer of 2001 the most unusual movie to hit the airwaves was "Final Fantasy." It starred Aki Ross, who looks a bit like a younger, sleeker Demi Moore. But Ross doesn't have the heart that Moore has. In fact, she has no heart at all. That's because Aki and the rest of the actors in Final Fantasy are digital figments of an animators creative imagination.

Final Fantasy is the first "cartoon" where the characters seem so lifelike that its female star wound up on the cover of a men's magazine. This feat of magic has Hollywood all in titters. Says Tom Hanks, "I am very troubled by it. But it's coming down man. It's going to happen and I'm not sure what actors can do about it."

Right now actors don't have much to worry about. Digital animators still need human beings to get the moves right and share their resonant voices. And directors and producers are bending over backwards to keep their human stars placated. Final Fantasy producer Chris Lee says that he used digital actors to save real actors' lives (that's a good one) in those daring stunts so common to today's story-line poor, but action-rich movies. Lee said that he specifically chose well-known character actors Donald Sutherland, Steve Buscemi and James Woods for their "warmth and resonance" to provide voices of the film's characters."

They needn't have bothered. The technology really does stand on its own. As one message board participant says, "The visual experience of the movie is outstanding. Landscapes, atmosphere, characters are incredible."

Technology really does have a way of jumping ahead in spurts. **In** mid-2001 AT&T Labs announced that they had invented technology to replicate any voice, any time. Want to record a commercial using Whoppi Goldberg's voice without having to fly Whoppi to your recording studio? Not to worry, this technology will extrapolate a new speech - complete with proper inflections and intonations - from a sample of Whoppi's voice.

Truth be told, few of us movie-goers would recognize a movie star's voice unless it were totally distinctive. Really - any voice would do. Alas, Hollywood moguls feel just the opposite and saddle their animated features with high costs of using name "voices". Just what's the story behind using celebrities in cartoons that only children will ever see?

One of the most talked about technological efforts of recent years was a film shot for Seattle's rock 'n roll museum. The film appears to be a performance by a young James Brown. It isn't. The filmmakers simply superimposed the performance of the current-day Brown, who dies in 2006, over a digital skeleton of the performer as a young man.

The Internet really does provide a whole new way to interact with our favorite form of entertainment - the movies. As an online strategy and web development expert for public and investor relations firm Makovsky Worldwide, Mike Sockol knows a thing about how we use the Internet for entertainment. As a civilian, always on the lookout for a fun thing to do, Mike can find much more fun using the Internet,

Because the Web aggregates information, there is little that I cannot learn about any movie that interests me. I particularly enjoy reading movie reviews. Before the Web, I would rely upon my local newspaper or maybe watch a review on TV. Now I go to E! Online and find multiple reviews from different sources all in one place. When the Internet sprang on the public consciousness, a lot of pundits stressed that this new medium changed everything. But in truth, the Web simply enhances existing media. Even though broadband promised a day when people will be able to watch movies through their computer screens, the Internet won't put movie theatres out of business. After all, the movie industry survived television for the same reason it will survive the Internet. Neither medium can provide the shared communal experience associated with seeing a movie with other people. It's going to be tough for the Web to duplicate the large screens, the booming sound systems, or even the smell of buttered popcorn.

Even more extensive for the film buff than E! Online is IMDb.com, formally known as the Internet Movie Database. It provides a comprehensive, searchable and cross-referenced directory listing almost every actor, directory, gaffer and best boy since 1891. It also lists plots, trivia, goofs and memorable quotes. It's the message boards, however, that provide the real scuttlebutt on the movie industry.

There's been more than a few instances of movie producers "loading" an ad with fictitious favorable comments from reviewers. In June of 2001 Terry Teachout, a music and movie critic for the New York Times, wrote a hilarious OpEd article about Sony Pictures creation of a fake reviewer to write highly enthusiastic blurbs about its movies. Teachout figured that he could license his name directly to the movie studio for use in ads so that you would not have to sit through *"hours of witless trash"*. Maybe, he ponders, Sony is onto something.

Perhaps Mr. Teachout doesn't realize it but there already are thousands, upon thousands of "virtual reviewers" out there. These are the folks that use the various movie site message boards or Rotten Tomatoes to tell others what they think of a particular movie (or book).

On the IMDb site here's what Zoe had to say about Battlefield Earth, a rather unfortunate movie starring the erstwhile John Travolta, which garnered only 2.3 out of 10 viewer stars,

Actually, was anyone involved with this all-out disaster thinking at all? My personal guess: no, and if they were, I'd rather not

know about what ..... Having heard what a start to finish mess this was .. .I decided to watch it, just for fun. Wow, was it plain unbelievable ... Horrible beyond all our expectations.

Zoe and her brother then go on to figure out just how the producers spent their reported 70 million dollar budget. Zoe figures on $40 million for Travolta, 24 million for special effects, costumes, sets, etc., about $5 million for additional salaries leaving just $112 and change for the script itself.

Needless to say, I didn't see the movie. I did take a peek at it one day, however, the sight of Travolta in dreadlocks so unnerved me that I turned off my TV for the remainder of the weekend.

Once you decide on a movie by reviewing what everyone else thinks of it and searching for incongruities on the nitpickers site, the next step is to usually go and see it. There's an AMC 16-plex about a mile away from where I live. If I'm desperate to see a movie that I think will sell out I can actually buy a ticket right on AMC's Internet site. Of course, I'll pay an extra buck for the privilege but at least I'll get into see the movie. I've never actually done this since there hasn't been a movie really worth waiting in line for since the first Star Wars was released back in the late 1970s. But I'm not everybody and there were at least 100,000 everybodies that bought "Hannibal" tickets over Moviefone.com's ticketing site.

There's no doubt that people like Movie sites. Internet movie ticketing sites have been visited by an estimated 10% of U.S. moviegoers. All of this is just so much extra publicity for the studios. Over the past few years most studios have been investing in movie web sites of their own for each feature that they produce. The king of all individual movie web sites and, in fact, the one that really started the whole trend was "The Blair Witch."

Blair Witch was a very, very low budget movie produced

by independents. Shot with a hand-held camera using a herky, jerky - grab your Dramamine - technique it wasn't the movie that generated all the buzz. It was the web site.

The web site was so compelling it virtually forced you into the movie theatres. That's because it wasn't your run of the mill ordinary "marketing" web site, instead it offered some interactive features that really piqued your interest. The movie became a sensation, spawning a sequel.

Blair Witch, and its various sequel, have been out for quite some time now. Like other studios, the one that distributes Blair Witch produced DVD versions of the flicks with additional footage to lengthen the life of the product. The new and improved version of the Blair Witch web site ties into all that by providing clues.

Perhaps the most intriguing use of the Internet as "bait" to lure viewers to see a particular movie came out of Steven Spielberg's studio for the movie A.I. Spielberg created some 20 "mystery" sites that, he hoped, would act like a trail of virtual breadcrumbs across the Web leading millions of moviegoers straight from their PCs to the box office.

One of these sites was familychan.org. It looked like any number of other personal family web sites. There were pictures of Evan and Nancy as well as their children. There was even information about where they worked. The thing about it is that the Chans - at least these Chans - don't exist. A careful reading of the site, and the hyperlinks to where they work, give you little hints about the future - as it appears in the movie. Evan works at fictitious company donu-tech.com which *"was the decisive voice in the decision against attempting to refloat San Francisco"*. In the movie A.I., which takes place in the distant future, most of the world is underwater due to climate change and the resulting meltdown of the icecaps. So it makes sense to see this bit of information on donu-tech's web site. I just wonder how many venture capitalists have wandered onto this high-tech web site and tried to contact the management team to invest money- it would be par for the course for this group of money vultures that, in reality, make investments in companies whose business plans were equally "pie in the sky".

For every web site created by a movie or television producer to hype a movie are two web sites with the goal of telling you the ending of the movie before anyone sees it. When the TV show Survivor first aired the producers made everyone involved sign a contract saying that they would never divulge

the winner's name while the series was airing Survivor pits person against person in a series of challenges on a remote tropical. Only one person would win the million dollars and millions of viewers tune in to see who will be booted off the island that week. The problem for the show's producers is that the survivorsucks.com web site had a nasty habit of spilling the beans before each show was aired.

Even endings of movies are no longer sacrosanct. Matt Drudge, famous for being the first to spill the beans about Bill and Monica, published the ending of "The Planet of the Apes" on drudgereport.com.

Sex has always sold - in any medium and in every era. Some say that the Internet has been virtual Viagra for the adult industry. Even when the Internet was still in diapers, back in 1998, online porn profits topped over $1 billion - up 30% from the year before.

There are hundreds of thousands of porn web sites online. Indeed porn is the most popular form of Internet on the Internet - and off. What makes Internet porn even more compelling to its aficionados is that they can spare themselves the embarrassment of being seen renting pornographic videos or going to X-rated movie theatres. It's all sex and all the time.

None of this is possible without having "actors" who

make these videos. Sad to say, that there is no lack of these mostly desperate people. One of these is Natalia, a young college student who is paying her own way using the money she earns working in the Internet sex trade,

My name is Natalia. I am a performer on the Internet. Customers can interact with me and tell me what to do. There are some strange people out there and we get them all. Most people don 't expect you to be educated and well-spoken. They expect a brainless little Barbie doll that they can play with - with moveable parts. It's a totally different side of people. This is a different side of me. If you saw me on the street you wouldn't know I do this. It's hard to find somebody that's going to respect you who's going to want a wife or girlfriend who masturbates on the Internet for other men to watch.

And, then there's gaming.

Dear Ann Landers,
About two years ago, my 57-year old wife staring playing a computer game. At first she would play a few times a week. Now it has taken over her whole life .....Not Winning in Wisconsin

"Not Winning" shouldn't feel bad. After porn, gambling is the most addictive entertainment on the Net, and this is an addiction shared equally by the sexes.

Brian McElvane and his Mississippi poker-playing buddies would road-trip to Biloxi every night, dig their elbows into the soft green felt at the Isle of Capri Casino, order up free beer and play Texas Hold 'em until dawn ..... Instead they grab their MasterCards and head to the virtual cardroom at paradisepoker.com ..... "staring at a monitor isn't near as much fun as actually seeing the guys with their poker pusses, bluffing ..... but we enjoy this online stuff".

The Pew Internet and American Life project estimates that more than 4.5 million Americans have gambled online at least once. Online gambling fever isn't limited to the U.S. alone. In the U.K. the one year growth of gaming sites) has more than doubled.

There are hundreds of happy campers who gamble online. Here's what Poppa Terry had to say on the Winner Online message board,

Just had to share this with you folks. I opened an account at Global Player Casino this evening. Put $50 on my credit card, got a $30 bonus .. . put in $50 ..... on my first hand I drew a full house. I said what the hell. Kept it at $5 and the next hand drew 4 sevens! Without passing "GO'~ I went to the cashier and out in a withdrawal for $600 ..... Now if I could do this all the time, I'd never have to work again ... "

Just who gambles online? UK-based Henley Centre found that online gamblers have a very different profile than traditional gamblers - they're computer literate and are of a higher social status than those who use bookmakers. The Henley study also found that people see online gambling as a way to escape from the pressures of everyday life. Given that we're working more hours than ever before one can expect that online gambling seems to have found itself an solid niche - particularly since this is one leisure activity you can actually do at work.

According to PC Magazine there are 1.8 billion gamers in the world. Back in the 1970s I used my primitive computer and the Basic programming language to craft a game I called Shark. The goal here was to retrieve the bag of gold before the shark pulled off your limbs and swallowed you. The artwork was crude and the immersion quite primitive. Today games such as Fortnite are immersing gamers in online artistically creative virtual worlds.

Art is my passion, I was brought up in a museum. Although I was reared in the less than prestigious borough of Queens, the skyline of Manhattan was no more than 50 yards away from my window. My father evidently loved museums so, like clockwork, each and every Sunday, from my earliest memories, he trundled my sister, myself and assorted pigtailed friends into the car for the trek across the "Great Divide" - the East River.

Thus the Metropolitan's basement, where all the Egyptian stuff was kept back then, was my basement, the cafeteria, my kitchen, and the great works of art no more threatening then the "starving artists" original oils that my mother hung up on the walls of our living room.

Museums are often called elitist and they probably are if the color of its patrons is considered. For the most part, at least in the NY area, those that hang around the Met, the Whitney and the Guggenheim are overwhelmingly white. Why should this be so? A case has been made that what's hanging (and standing) in most museums has been created by white hands and, thus, not relevant to the non-white experience. This is referred to as the "dead white male" syndrome - the term created in response to the debate concerning which authors and poets to assign to freshman English students (Walt Whitman - dead white poet so Nyet to him). Well, I might be white but I'm certainly not male (and thankfully not dead yet) so this doesn't apply to me. In my opinion, art transcends all divides. It's not white, not black and not brown. It just is.

Having been a city girl, surrounded by art at every turn, I was unprepared for the drought when I moved to the suburbs in my fourth decade. Lush rolling landscapes, a mall every quarter mile and the occasional tiny antiques town are no substitute for city living where art seems to infused on every street corner and you can walk for miles without seeing the same thing twice (except for the regular intervals of Starbucks, the Gap and Pinki Nail Salons).

The suburbs has no culture. I used to think that the reason for this was that most folks preferred to go "into the city" for their culture, but now I'm not so sure. If suburbanites wanted museums, then there would be museums. Of course, there are the scattered cultural institutions - a mini-museum here, a theatre group there but there's little that's world class out in the suburbs. Just how does these folks survive?

From what I can see, they go to work, watch their kids play soccer and then putter around their houses after spending an hour or two at the mall. I may be a culture snob, but I'm right. How can we fix this?

I always thought that a good way to remedy this situation would be to require mall builders to allot one or two "stores" as free or subsidized spaces for the arts. So you can go to Macys, but also see a play. You can return that wrench to Sears and still have enough time to catch the new Hudson Valley Retrospective.

Surburbanites who need to flex those cultural brain cells and snotty urbanites with a penchant for saying "been there, done that" can just go online. The Web Gallery of Art is a good place to start (https://www.wga.hu/). The Web Gallery of Art contains thousands of digital reproductions of European paintings and sculptures created between the years 1150 and 1800. You can either look at the images individually or take one of the guided tours.

I decided to grab my camera (oh wait, I don't need a camera) and head for Tour #8 which was "Art in Siena: 13th - 16th centuries". Virtually, I learned a bit about Siena, the Sienese school of painting as well as the Viennese school of sculpture. After this quick intro, I took a more detailed tour of Sienese painters and learned about the techniques of painters such as Coppo Di Marcovaldo and Simone Martini - painters I hadn't noticed in the vast Metropolitan Museum of Art in New York.

If you're a Canadian - or just interested in Canadian art and heritage - then it might be worthwhile for you to visit the Virtual Museum of Canada (http://www.virtualmuseum.ca) where you can create your very own virtual museum composed of anyone or more objects located on the web site. I'm rather partial to Inuit sculpture so I filled my bucket, so to speak, with delightful images or caribou and artic birds.

There are hundreds of virtual museums, most have just text and images, but more than a few are highly intensive webcasting experiences. You can visit the Yerkes astronomy observatory or discover some interesting fossils found in Santa Cruz County of California. Most museums today do have a virtual presence.

The most intriguing aspect of virtual museuming is that, collector willing, you can get an inside look at stuff you'd never see in a traditional museum. Take "Paul's Virtual Museum." About four thousand folks have visited U.K.-based Paul's museum of obsolete technology like the Pathescope Son, 9.5mm Optical Sound film projector that came out in 1951.. .. .I think I may actually have something like this in my attic!

You can visit museums and look at and learn about art online. Armchair enthusiasts, particularly those geographically distanced from major cultural centers, can do a whole lot more.

I have great interest in archaeology. I subscribe to most of the major magazines in the field and try to travel to as many ancient places as I can. But I can't go everywhere and since I didn't take these courses in college I don't know a whole lot about the science of archaeology. That's where the Internet comes in. For example, I can travel to the Archaelogical Institute of America's Interactive Digs website (https://www.interactivedigs.com/) and roll up my sleeves.

Music lovers are always looking for the next best thing. So are the record companies. But the record companies have short attention spans when it comes to new bands today. If you're a musician your music has to make the top ten on the first attempt or your record company will drop you like a hot potato. I'm not quite sure that even the Beatles would be produced today.

Producing yourself might be the only option for the truly gifted today. Fortunately, the Internet provides just that sort of independence. Soundcloud and Apple's iTunes are just two examples of platforms that allow just about anyone to upload their creations and get paid for it.

The person who really jump-started the Internet music revolution was a teenager by the name of Shawn Fanning. This kid created the Napster program which permitted music lovers to share their music libraries. Long since gone legit due to a ruling that Napster violated copyright laws, the idea of music file sharing spawned a great deal of controversy.

As a music publisher I am disgusted by people using Napster .. Do the people who use it not have brains? If no one gets paid then there's not going to be any new music coming out. Artists struggle to make ends meet in the first place, the arrival of Napster makes it harder. Napster users' enthusiasm for downloading music is admirable but if these people want to be downloading new music in a few years they better stop using illegal sites like Napster.

For every person who feels the way this music publisher feels another thinks just the opposite.

The whole Napster thing is crap. Don't tell me that there isn't one person in the whole world who hasn't got a blank cassette with music recorded onto it, either off an album or off the radio. So anyone who disses Napster is a hypocrite.

There's a big brouhaha brewing and it's been brewing for some time. While Napster has resurrected itself as an online music seller, there are dozens of
Napster-clones online all enabling music lovers to download free music. Unknown independents will continue to use the Internet to create a presence for themselves as well as to sell

their wares. The majors will use it for marketing and the music lovers will continue scrounging around the Internet looking for the new, the cool and the (hopefully) free.

I think the market will level out with smaller labels using the web cleverly to improve their physical sales. And the majors doing what they always do - selling shit loads of cheesy pop. I think people will still get free music which may take away some physical sales. Nobody knows what will happen. It's the future after all.

For more than two years a big chunk of web devotees were caught up in the story of Kaycee Nicole. Kaycee was a pretty student who was dying from leukemia. She kept people updated via her online diary. Her mother also kept a companion diary to express the feelings associated with caring for a child with cancer. Thousands of people who read these diaries corresponded with Kaycee through email, chat and even phone conversations.

When Kaycee's Mom informed everyone that Kaycee had finally succumbed to this disease, her online friends grieved like they had lost members of their own families. The thing of it is that Kaycee never died. In fact, she never even existed. The story was the figment of imagination of a mother and daughter with a lot of time on their hands, fraud in their hearts, and a way with words.

Kelli Swenson was a middle schooler in the Oklahoma City metro area. Kelli and several of her friends created a website for an imaginary girl named Kaycee Nicole in 1997 or 1998. They used pictures of a local high school basketball star to give Kaycee the face of an attractive young girl. At some point, Kelli's mother Debbie decided to take over the "game" and by giving Kaycee leukemia turned it into a full-fledged hoax. Somewhere around this time, Kaycee joined the College Club website where she became a popular member of the community. Kaycee was even quoted in a New York Times article about college life. Kaycee's blog became popular.

The love and fearlessness displayed by a dying girl was inspirational. Debbie weaved a tale of remission and reoccurrence that kept well wishers locked on to the site. As imaginary Kaycee's overall condition deteriorated, her friends sent cards, gifts and possibly money. After a few years Debbie decided that this had dragged on long enough. Just when Kaycee looked to be beating cancer, Debbie said she had an aneurysm and died. The community outpouring of support was remarkable and those who knew Kaycee suffered serious bouts of grief. This is when folks *become* suspicious. Debbie refused to provide an address to send cards or condolences and would not provide any real information about a funeral.

This web hoax duped a lot of people One of those was Randall van der Woning from Hong Kong. He was so moved by Kaycee's story that he offered to design and host her weblog at his own expense,

I never wanted to play up being the victim. But the simple truth is I have been victimized just like many others have .... I'm dealing with embarrassment, betrayal, anger, regret and disappointment. I felt worry, anxiety, fear, dread, sorrow, and grief. I lost Kaycee when she died and I lost her again when I learned she was a phantom .... I have not been able to sleep properly. I have not eaten much. I have the shakes. I have headaches. I'm physically, mentally and emotionally exhausted. In order to develop relationships, whether online or in person, one must be willing to trust. My sense of trust most certainly has been violated. I opened my heart and, for a year I gave of my time, money, energy, emotional and spiritual resources to help someone, an in the end, I was burned for it.

Blogging is a popular pastime on the Internet. Many have no semblance to reality. And a few go the route of full hoax like Kaycee Nicole. Still there are some that would like to an enforce strict standard of making people prove who they really are. But, of course, this is quite counter to the prevailing culture on the web.

The web lets you be who you want to be. If you're an unhappily married, fat postal worker you can feel free to live your life online as a svelte supermodel or brainy nuclear physicist. On the other hand, if you're a svelte supermodel with an actual brain you can use the web to hide your physical assets and just let folks enjoy you for the "real you."

Then there are those people who want to communicate but need to do so under the cloak of protective anonymity - like Afghan women protesting their treatment under the Taliban or Tibetan monks protesting China's rule of their homeland.

Some people, like Jessica W., use blogs in lieu of the Freudian talking cure,

I am still tired. The one thing that I really wanted this weekend (to get some sleep) and I did not get [it]. Of course I am going to crash hard this week. I have so much to do and it is all my fault for being a procrastinator. I think that I will be able to have a productive weekend if I can get through this week without any incidents. So far so good. JO is not here today. Horrible side effect from faking, paranoia. So bad, that it is lapsing into other parts of my life. I will get through this., I will get through this okay.

A lot of what's on the web, unfortunately, appears to be stream of consciousness - unreadable, incoherent and, quite frankly, disappointingly dull. The "personal" web does not have editors.

I was young and needed the money ..... Yes Jerwin, this is that Guy who blogged for a while then gave up, telling everyone to go outside and "smell flowers" around June last year. Firstly, very embarrassing .... 'Pick up a flower. Smell it. say "arghhh" .... What

did I mean? I don't know

The next step up the writers' food chain from blogging is vanity publishing. Companies like Vantage Press have been around for years, but then Amazon entered the fray. Vanity publishing is now on steroids.

Alan Winter is a periodontist but he'd rather be writing. After he wrote "Snowflakes in the Sahara", and after being rejected by every legitimate publisher and literary agent in town Dr. Winter decided to use iUniverse, Barnes & Noble's Internet-publishing partner. He paid $299 for iUniverse's Showcase evaluation of his book, $300 for editing and $5,000 on buying books for signings and to send to reviewers. He pays about $15 for each book that he sells for $23.95. But vanity book authors just can't get "no respect,"

I think this book is as worthy as any out there. But people can't believe that a dentist is capable of writing fiction. Publishing it by a vanity press was my biggest mistake. I'm a serious writer, and people don't look at vanity press authors as serious .. I'm disenchanted.

The vast majority of Internet users do not publish blogs, pull hoaxes or author novels - but do like to talk. The anonymity of the online world lets you say things that you would never say face to face. This is both good and bad. A Pew study found that 37% of teens use the Internet to write something they would not have said in person. "That's what the Internet's for - slandering others anonymously", said one of characters in the summer-lite comedy "Jay and Silent Bob Strike Back".

There are virtually thousands of Facebook and Reddit groups all yaking away about topics as diverse as Cajun cooking to alien invasion. Insults levied, screaming is common and emotions are often raw.

I poured through thousands of message board messages when doing research for this book and, while many were intelligent and literate, most were ill-tempered and quasi-illiterate. That famous internet anonymity really does breed contempt as well as a rare form of educational amnesia causing a forgetfulness on how to use spelling, punctuation and grammar.

Many of us use the Internet to just while away time - sort of like starring into space. Starring at a glowing monitor can be quite mesmerizing. But ever the hyperactive folks that we are, our fingers just seem to drawn to the keyboard.

When the brain's on low fuel the last place we want to surf to is an high-octane site so instead we surf to those mindless sites that seem to make up a significant portion of the web. In St. Louis, Brian Gottlieb has wired his telephone to display to Internet users the hour and date of his most recent phone call. Paul Haas in Michigan has hooked a computer to his refrigerator and hot tub to report their respective temperatures. In Pittsburgh, Michael Witbrock uses a voice synthesizer to let online visitors "talk" to the cat that likes to sleep in the warmth of his modem.

Sleeping pill, anyone?

@HEALTH

Remember Jessica W., our "talking cure" blogger, from the previous chapter?

I am still tired. The one thing that I really wanted this weekend (to get some sleep) and I did not get [it}. Of course I am going to crash hard this week. I have so much to do and it is all my fault for being a procrastinator. I think that I will be able to have a productive weekend if I can get through this week without any incidents. So far so good. JO is not here today. Horrible side effect from faking, paranoia. So bad, that it is lapsing into other parts of my life. I will get through this., I will get through this okay.

Jessica W. Is one of 100 million Americanss who use the Internet to make themselves, or a family member, feel better. Of course, Jessica probably didn't realize that her blog was being interpreted as a plea for help - but it is. For Jessica, just the act of spilling her guts out online was cathartic and therefore therapeutic.

Harvey Asher is a psychiatrist extraordinaire.. He sees a real value to the Internet for mental health reasons,

What we can say is that people no longer have to feel alone. Because of the shame of it, because of the way society reacts, there is a tendency for people with mental health difficulties to feel isolated.

Finding other people - even seeing it written about - takes some of that shame and isolation away. Examples of this include: someone who is experiencing post-traumatic disorder because of serving in the Armed Forces; or someone who's been sexually abused as a child. It's like everything comes out of the closet by just putting the words into a search engine.

So information is one aspect of the value of the Internet in the mental health field. Another aspect is finding other people through chats that you can share your problems with .... It's being anonymous .... it's almost as if you have the same spiritual approach that you find in Alcoholics Anonymous. You can share with other people, know that you are not unique and yet have that spiritual flow .

People with severe health problems are at an advantage with the 'Net since they can find out about drug interactions and side effects even if it happens to be accidentally minimized by their health professional they are working with or if they were embarrassed to ask detailed questions of their health professional. On the other side of the equation, however, they can get so much information they can get frightened. The good news is that they can go back to the Internet if frightened about the medication and talk to people who've been on the same medication.

On a personal level- I'm interested in magnetic therapy. While at the park with my granddaughter I met a woman with her child who had Cerebral Palsy. I told her about the therapy and called her later. She had already looked it up on the Internet, found people who had used magnets for children with Cerebral Palsy and was able to talk to me in a very enlightened way ....

There's a real boom in using the Internet for health related purposes. Perhaps we're all cyberchondriacs. Or maybe it's just a logical continuation of the health fad which started more than a decade ago. Baby boomers, getting on in years, started to take exercise and good eating habits seriously. Health club memberships soared as well as sales of in-home exercise equipment and restaurants starting offering "Free" menus - i.e. no-fat and no-cholesterol.

According to a survey released by the Pew Internet and American Life Project 55 percent of Internet users used the Internet to gather medical information. One of these people is Pam Kipreos who went to the Web in search of weight loss information for a friend and treatment options for ovarian cancer for her mother.

Two decades ago Americans rarely trudged to the library to look up the minor medical conditions that they had - or thought they had. Instead, they trusted their age- and experienced-wizened family doc and whatever specialists he (and it usually was a he) brought in.

Several things have changed since then. First, the pace of scientific and medical discovery has accelerated. A spate of new - or rather old but lurking in the shadows of known science - diseases have been discovered. AIDs, HIV, West Nile, Ebola, ZIKA ad, now, EEE are just some of their dreaded names. Many of these diseases were hidden away in isolated and remote corners of the earth, but the advent of globalization and rapid airplane transit, has opened the floodgates to ancient scourges in the new world.

Scientists have not been letting the moss grow either. Astonishing discoveries have been made - the decipherment of the human genome being just the last of this long and exciting list. The pharmaceuticals have followed every discovery with the announcement of "new and improved" drugs for everything from schizophrenia to heart disease.

Perhaps the most dramatic change has been the way health care is being delivered - at least in the United States. Managed care became the mainstream method of health care delivery, during this period, because American corporations could no longer afford to foot the bill for ever-escalating health care costs. This coupled with a tightening of the Medicare budget has led to a double whammy for Doctors - reduced income and more patients. Doctors are not happy campers.

If doctors are unhappy then health consumers are miserable. A quick survey of my family and friends tells me that waits are ever longer in the waiting room while the visits themselves are short with the Doctor being more and more distracted. Drs. Kildare and Welby have retired and in their place is someone who doesn't know you, hasn't the time to really listen to you, and sometimes makes mistakes. My own cousin's husband, a chief surgeon in a leading hospital in New York City, tells me that he doesn't visit other doctors. "I've seen too much," he tells me referring to the mistakes and cut corners he sees on a day to day basis. The only weapon a patient has, nowadays, is his or her knowledge about what ails him. Increasingly, that knowledge is coming from the Internet.

There are thousands of health-related web sites online today. One need only type a term into a search engine and you'll be whisked away to any number of informational - and not so informational - sites. For example, I typed "acne" into a search engine and had 197 million sites returned to me. I'm sure that the vast majority of these sites were for commercial purposes. After all, the web was popularized by commerce so it's understandable that these web sites have an ulterior motive - to sell you something.

At the end of 2000 my father was rushed to a hospital. It turns out that he needed an aortic valve replacement as well as a double bypass. This he had but he made very slow progress in his recovery worrying myself, my mother and my sister. While age was certainly a consideration – he was 85 - my family needed constant reassurance that he was going to get better. We wanted our old Dad back.

For those who have experienced this sort of thing first-hand, you'll commiserate with our confusion. Everyone told us a different story. His heart surgeon, whose credentials I had checked out on the Web, had the best story. He assured us that he'd snap back to normal and he was ultimately right. But not everyone was so reassuring. We got a wide variety of opinions - of varying degrees of optimism - from his two cardiologists, his neurologist, his geriatric doctor, the physician assistant, etc. etc. etc.

At that point I needed some support. For this I turned to one of the many discussion groups that live on the Web. It was here that I finally got some reassurance that it could take many months to snap back to normal.

Most of us have aches and pains and some of us have real problems. We often procrastinate before going to a doctor, usually opting to discuss our symptoms around the dinner table or water cooler. Misery loves company so it's reassuring to find that you're not the only one who's every had a ringing in the ears or itchy throat. But there's a limit to the number of people around that dinner table or water cooler. The Internet's water cooler, on the other hand, has room for millions.

Mark Veverka has been suffering from back pain for over 16 years. Those with the same affliction know that there are various forms of treatment for this sort of problem. There's traditional medicine which relies on pills and surgery, then there are chiropractors who rely on spinal manipulation and those Eastern treatments such as acupuncture. Needless to say, the first group holds the other groups up for ridicule. Says Veverka, "back patients have traditionally been twisting in the wind. Not to mention writhing with pain"

Veverka had already decided against going under the knife thanks to the personal accounts of the trials and tribulations of back surgery. That still left him twisting in the wind, so he decided to go the Internet to do a bit of research. His research would have uncovered information on Canadian deep muscle massage or the Maitland technique. The treatment that most intrigued Veverka was something called Vertical Axial Decompression - or VAX.D . VAX. - D is sort of a modern day rack that pulls the vertebrae apart. VAX.-D has its own web site (www.vaxd.net) and its own bulletin board were back pain suffers gather to discuss this novel form of treatment, like this message from Ron,

1 am a 35 year old truck driver. 1 have suffered with low back pain and pain in my legs since 1 was in my teens. 1 have sought treatment   and every time 1 was told it was due to weak muscles   that physical therapy would fix me right up. It didn't. I requested that x-rays be taken but I was told that they weren't needed because doctors had seen this problem many times over .... I got older and the pain became worse .. .! didn't even want to get out of bed in the morning.

Then Ron found VAX-D and he thinks he's getting better. Ron's positive comments encouraged other folks to go for the same treatment.

Sometimes the result of your search are less than encouraging - frightening even. When Veronica Rippe typed in the keywords: pain, fever, kidney, cyst the search engine turned up a bunch of websites all, alarmingly, on polycystic kidney disease. Most of these sites described the disease as potentially fatal. In tears, Veronica called her doctor who told her that what she had was serious but wasn't polycystic kidney disease and she wasn't going to die.

Thank goodness. Sometimes, however, what you find on the Internet does indeed match your problem and can save your life. This happened to Tara DelGado who was suffering from a fever and sharp pains in her side. She wanted to wait until morning to contact a doctor but her brother-in-law, who had gone online and found a checklist indicating that Tara might have appendicitis, convinced her to go to the emergency room. She had her appendix removed that night.

Harried doctors love it when you come armed with your Internet research printouts. Most feel that the patients who have done extensive searches are often well informed and you can spend less time on the basics and more time on the finer points of treatment. Because it provides links around the world, the Internet can be an especially valuable source of information for people with rare or difficult conditions. One man had several surgeries for recurrent respiratory papilloma. After his third surgery, he sent an e-mail query that led him to learn about several remedies his doctor had never heard of, remedies that aborted the growth of his polyps.

There are hundreds of thousands of health-related sites to choose from. Many of these sites are inaccurate and incomplete. At one point, the California Health Care Foundation published a study in the Journal of the American Medical Association rating some of these sites on the difficulty of finding information and the site's accuracy and completeness. The study involved Internet information on breast cancer, childhood asthma, depression and obesity. The study found that sites offered complete and accurate information on breast cancer 63% of the site; 36% for childhood asthma; 44% for depression; and 37% for obesity.

The August 1999 issue of the medical journal Cancer had an even bleaker report. Of the 371 websites about Ewing's sarcoma, which is a rare bone cancer, 42% contained medical information that had not been subjected to stringent scientific review, and 6% contained outright inaccuracies.

The caveat here is that you can't just trust one website. Like in the real world - it's best to get a second opinion. It's also a good idea to utilize only sites that are credible such as those that adhere to Health on the Net Foundation's voluntary code of conduct.

While some sites contain inaccuracies and distortions

these are not put there deliberately. Usually, it's general sloppiness or just the enormity of the amount of information to be inputted and updated that causes the problem. There are some places on the Internet, however, that deliberately supply misinformation and are very dangerous to your health.

Anorexia is a modern day psychological scourge. Countless thousands of young women, influenced by rail thin supermodels, movie and television stars such as the emaciated - and none too pleasant looking - Calista Flockhart of Ally McBeal fame, are starving themselves to death.

The Internet, ever free in its first amendment right to say anything, hosts hundreds of underground web sites supportive of this self-abusive life style. Led by defiant young women in denial, these sites resolve around the idea that anorexia should be embraced and even supported.

Daniel le Grange, Joint Director of the Eating Disorders Program University of California San Francisco Benioff Children's Hospital, reviewed a number of these pro-anorexia sites,

I thought, my God, what is this? I couldn't believe what I was seeing. Patients who don't understand the full extent of their illness, that's nothing new. But bonding together to teach people over the Internet how to become better anorexics, I've never come across anything like this before.

One of these sites is Anorexic Nation which, reminds you that freedom of expression is an inalienable right. Here you're confronted with a series of skeletal images of a young girl that would make an Auschwitz survivor look like they had meat on their bones. The rest of the site is devoted to the principles of losing weight by fasting and even purging.

CyberAnoerexics celebrate their conditions, usually proclaiming that it is a lifestyle decision and not an illness to be fixed. However, if you read some of their postings you find it's anything but a lifestyle. Here's what KittyStrawberry had to say when passing through the S.C.aR.E.D Eating Disorder Message Forum,

I was just passing by this website and happen to see this forum .. Well it been a long time since I visited. Let me tell you something about me. I am pro-anorexia .. I have been pro-anorexia since March. And so you are going to ask me: what about my precious life?? What about the future?? What about my plan to get married and have beautiful children?? Let me remind you, I don't want to die and I aren't going to die .. I don't even care about any of that when it comes to being thin. I would give up my life in a heartbeat just to be thin. Let me correct you, I am not pro-anorexia because I want to die. I am pro-anorexia because I want to be thin. I want to be thin because I want to feel perfect...

These girls think of anorexia as their friend. They've even given it a name - Ana.

My most happy and successful memories are from when I was a successful anorexic ... God, I want to be there again ... I want to be empty and clean and free again .... So, thankfully, ana has re-entered my life.

There's a lot of pain out there and much of it is reflected in writings on the web - open for all to see. Sometimes, however, there is a real danger to showing too much of yourself as Jaeyde explains,

Have you ever thought there are some things that you really should just keep to yourself? Because sometimes no good ever comes from telling someone what you're really thinking ... A couple of years back I was on the receiving end of hate mail from an anti-abortion group. I'm not sure where it came from, why they picked on me, after all I never exactly accepted that I'd done the right thing, in fact it was something that caused me a whole lot of pain and confusion. I had an abortion because I was pregnant from being raped.

There are many people with much emotional and physical baggage out there in the ether. Some like, Jaeyde, post their feelings and experiences online. Some prefer to lurk in the shadows and read what others have posted - gaining strength by knowing that there are others out there with much the same problems and experiences.

Still others out there take a more proactive approach and actually seek out a doctor that they can "see" online. For people who find it difficult to reach a doctor, or are too busy, worried or even embarrassed to go to their own general practitioner, there are now a wide variety of "tele" doctors for you to see online.

Dr. Tom Caffrey is a board certified physician as well as one of the founders of CyberDoc. Founded in 1996, but now offline. CyberDocs.com provided everything that Dr. Ash can only dream about and health consumers salivate over,

A patient comes online to our site and picks from a list of doctors. Each one is board certified Patients have a choice of either video web conferencing or chat. You can login and get an emergency medical specialist. He would be able to give you a good differential diagnosis - what you may or may not have.In the future we'll even be able to use home monitoring devices for blood pressure, temperature ...

Dr. Caffrey's service might be offline but medical centers are picking up the slack. Robert Wood Johnson Barnabas Health, a massive medical center in New Jersey, has been advertising their iPhone RWJBarnabas Health TeleMed app.

The Doctor is Online – RWJBarnabas Health TeleMed is a convenient, low-cost option for urgent medical care services, delivered online 24/7/365. Connect with a board-certified physician, immediately, from your home or while away for consultation, diagnosis and prescriptions (when appropriate) for common health complaints. No appointments, no long waits. Providers have an average of 10 to 15 years in urgent care, emergency, family, or primary care medicine, and are certified specifically in telehealth. It's easy and private – compliant with the Health Insurance Portability and Accountability Act (HIPAA). Simply log in to initiate a physician visit. No appointments and no long wait times. RWJBarnabas Health TeleMed brings healthcare home so you can feel better, faster.

Sometimes, however, the answers you get from telemedicine is anything but reassuring. Liz Sinclair's had some unusual symptoms. Since the age of 17 she had been having a frightening paralysis when lying down. While still conscious of all that was going on around her, she became unable to move or speak. She never consulted a doctor because she was too embarrassed by the symptoms and they were brief and infrequent.

Liz researched the condition on the Web and found that her condition might be something called sleep paralysis. Not being content with just researching the condition, Liz decided to visit a cyber doctor. The doctor suggested two possibilities: sleep paralysis or epilepsy, and said she should see a neurologist and have some tests. Said Liz, "I thought the answer was a little scary. I have had a test for epilepsy, so I know I haven't got that. Otherwise, his answer would have panicked me."

When you visit a "live" doctor you probably get a warm and fuzzy feeling just by being in the same room as the doctor. If you should meet with him in his private office, you might even see all his/her diplomas on the wall. The same cannot be said for a cyberdoc and, in fact, the laws are so vague about this that it's "caveat emptor" if you should choose to use these services.

Most off-line doctors today think that you should try to avoid giving health advice over Internet. They feel that it's a bit like doing a telephone diagnosis, which all doctors are wary of unless they can follow it up. Ultimately, once a doctor had given a patient medical advice, he or she has assumed a medical responsibility for the patient. One doctor I spoke to said that it was difficult for him to imagine that any physician is doing this for other than monetary return. He goes on to say that the whole contractual relationship between a doctor and a patient is that you actually see, touch, feel, smell a patient to get as much data as you can to be accurate in your diagnosis and treatment,

Part of the problem is that for every legitimate online health service, there are ten not so legitimate health services bamboozling their way across the Internet. Many of these are related to the sale of the so called lifestyle drugs like Viagra. In this gray area of medical science even good doctors can get roped in.

Dr. Leandro Pasos was struggling to make a living when he saw an advertisement that caught his eye. It said that doctors could earn up to $10,000 a month doing fully automated online medical reviews. The medical reviews were for a company that set up shop online to sell Viagra, the pill that offers men the hope of better sex through chemistry.

Dr. Pasos was an orthopedic surgeon and did not specialize or even know anything about impotence. But for $5,000 a month he agreed to review questionnaires sent electronically by prospective Viagra patients, authorizing prescriptions as he saw fit. This one act got the good doctor into a whole bunch of trouble with the Washington Medical Quality Assurance Commission, which cited him for unprofessional conduct for prescribing drugs to people he hadn't physically examined. Dr. Pasos' excuse - "I needed a job."

Drugs, it would seen, are the big winner so far on the Internet.

Everyone takes pills. Whether it's an antibiotic for that little infection, or a cholesterol-blocking drug or an anxiety reducing drug, we're all on something. We suffer from what is referred to as medical care inflation every year. According to the U.S. Bureau of Labor Statistics, prices for medical care were 89.42% higher in 2019 versus 2000 (a $894.22 difference in value). Obviously, there's something out of whack here. What's out of whack is the healthcare industry which I define as a combination of the medical, insurance and pharmaceutical industries.

Forty or so years ago we were all treated by kindly old gray hair doctors who sometimes took a rooster in trade for some medical treatment. With the advent of Medicare and employer-driven medical insurance, physicians developed an unhealthy profit motive that was often at odds with the Hippocratic oath. Before 1960, while physicians were more than middle class, there were few "rich" doctors. When insurance was introduced doctors somehow pushed themselves into the upper stratosphere of high income individuals - at least in the United States. Gone was Dr. Welby and in his place was a Jaguar-driving, mansion owning mini-corporation.

At the same time there was an explosion in what I like to refer to as health care inventions. These were pharmaceuticals (i.e. cholesterol-lowering drugs, HIV inhibitors, etc. and diagnostic devices such as MRIs.) Protected by medical insurance which paid for everything, consumers no longer needed to shop around to find the lowest price or, at least, someone to take their rooster. Physicians also no longer needed to worry about cost. They could treat and prescribe virtually anything and be assured that they would get paid.

In the early 1980s employers decided to reign in these ever-burgeoning medical costs and starting migrating their employees en masse over to managed care. I'm sure I don't need to explain what the effect of this was, suffice it to say that the reduction in cost was dramatic.

Insurance companies cut big deals with big employers which lowered premiums considerably. Of course, small businesses like mine, had no such clout and often wound up paying far higher premiums that did the large companies. Recently, even managed care premiums have begun to rise. The industry has already squeezed every last nickel out of the efficiencies of the managed care formula and it has nowhere else to squeeze. In addition, costs are rising. One of these costs is drugs.

Sometime in the late 1990's the government repealed its ban on drug advertising and the pharmaceuticals jumped into the arena with guns blazing. Now, advertising could be targeted directly at the consumer. And the consumer was ripe for the pitch. Seemingly hanging on every word, they marched into their doctors' offices and demanded the "drug of the day."

Advertising costs money, so does development of these new drugs. It also doesn't help that some third world countries have pressured the pharmaceutical industry to lower the costs of some drugs. In addition, the industry seems to have an interesting price structure so that you can travel to Tijuana in Mexico and buy a prescription drug for up to 40% cheaper than you can in this country. So we have several reasons why drugs cost so much: 1) advertising; 2) losses due to third world countries; 3) discount prices to some foreign countries. All of this boosts the price in this country. You can say that the American consumer is subsidizing the cost of drugs for the rest of the world.

Now that managed care has dashed most of our hopes for good and inexpensive health care, consumers are back on the market for good but affordable health care. They've turned to the Internet en masse, not to visit doctors online, but to try to buy discount drugs online. And there's no lack of places for them to go.

Virtually every major drug store chain has developed an online presence. There are hundreds of web sites that sell prescription drugs. Some, however, are considered "rogue sites." Widely reported cases of abuse include a 52-year old Illinois man who died of a heart attack after he took Viagra, which he ordered over the Internet. Although the death could not be conclusively tied to Viagra, reports state that the man had a family history of heart trouble that should have been taken into consideration before allowing him to get the prescription drug.

Pressure is mounting for stiffer government regulation for Internet drug sales. Of particular concern are sales from foreign based operations that don't bow to U.S. laws.

Companies like pharmagroup.com permit you to buy a wide variety of drugs - all prescription free although their site displays a bunch of disclaimers which describe possible confiscation of your shipment by custom authorities. It should be noted that foreign drug formularies are quite different from American. In other words, you won't get an American brand name drug. You will get the European brand name or generic equivalent, however.

While some contend that "face to face" contact and advice of the pharmacist cannot be digitized without serious consequences for the patient, the truth of the matter is that cyber-pharmacies are here to stay - for the cost, the convenience and, for some, the lack of any alternatives.

In 1999 Saint Louis University law professor Nicolas Terry published an article on "Cyber-Malpractice: Legal Exposure for Cybermedicine". His goal was to look at cybermedicine from the legal perspective of what constitutes cyber-malpractice. He described cybermedicine as health care providers operating in cyberspace - the migrations by health care providers, insurance companies, and drug companies to set up a practice or e-commerce on the Internet. He concluded that,

While telemedicine has already attracted the attention of legal scholars, this is nothing compared to the likely development of

cybermedicine and cyber-malpractice. The expansion of health care providers into virtual space will fundamentally change their methods of operation, their relationships with peer providers and patients and the type of interaction in which they indulge. Provider choices of business models, combined with the novelty of many of the malpractice-like claims that will result, will wreak a sea change in health care provider liability law, a changing risk allocation that likely will also reverberate in real space.

We all know that we're living in a very public world. They've got our number. The "they" is virtually everyone from - credit bureaus to employers - which makes it quite easy to perpetuate the burgeoning crime of identity fraud. While identity fraud is bad enough, add public access to your medical records and you'll need the services of a psychiatrist to get over the trauma.

Online is ripe for privacy leakage. First of all, for it to work implies that each medical provider (i.e. pharmacy, labs, etc.) has to have the ability to securely transport your data through the network. It's open to debate whether all these diverse entities can work together to achieve a secure enough environment (it's rather up in the air for even one to have this level of security in their external systems).

Pharmacies, labs, hospitals all keep records but these records are usually stored on an internal system where security leakages can be minimized. Once you open the data channel up for transport, you open the way for hackers to get into your system as well as pull data out of your system.

Today health information often leaks out of the system even when the privacy of a medical record appears to be intact. Expectant mothers, for example, are routinely bombarded by offers for magazines, baby formula, bottles, even when they don't remember signing up for them.

Despite new federal regulations that went into effect in

April of 2001, health records remain less private than most people think. Robert Gellman is a privacy expert based in Washington who seems to think that we have decided to give up our privacy,

In many ways health records are not confidential, because of decisions we have made as a society about the kind of health care we want. We have decided we want public health, so we allow people to be tracked and treated. We have decided we want research, and researchers need access to records. We have decided we want third-party payment; someone else pays your bill, and that someone is frequently your employer.

Actually we have decided nothing of the sort. What public health? And why are researchers being given access to my medical records for research that I did not agree to be part of? As far as my employer is concerned, just what right do they have to review any medical records?

All of this is dangerous stuff. Medical privacy is of vital concern to Americans. A national survey done for the California HealthCare Foundation found that one in every five people believes that an insurer, employer or health plan has already improperly gained access to their personal medical information.

This same study found that we're doing awfully strange things to protect our privacy - like using several doctors so that no one would have a complete record on them, to paying cash for care instead of submitting an insurance claim. Some even forego medical care lest their employers found out about a particular condition.

In July of 2001, the Association of American Physicians and Surgeons (AAPS) released results from a survey of 344 of their members showing that "patients are withholding information, and doctors are lying because of privacy concerns." AAPS found that nearly 87% of the physicians reported that a patient had asked that information be kept out of the patient's records, 78% reported withholding information from a patient's record at the patient's request due to privacy concerns, and 19% admitted to lying to protect a patient's privacy.

Even the Health Insurance Portability and Accountability Act places almost no limitations on some uses of medical information. For example, public health agencies are permitted to track the partners of those diagnosed with sexually transmitted diseases in order to get them into treatment - including HIV. Under these regulations, details of records can also be released for research if they are de-identified. They can also be used for marketing and fund-raising purposes.

Drug company collection of marketing information has become so widespread that some members of the AMA asked the organization to mount a protest. Doctors complained that drug companies were compiling lists of prescriptions they wrote for specific drugs and then bombarding patients with unsolicited mailings.

The ill effects of this free-flow of information are rather chilling and written about often in the press. In spite of these horror stories little has changed, or is expected to change.

Terri Seargent, a North Carolina resident, was fired from her job after being diagnosed with a genetic disorder that required expensive treatment. Three weeks before being fired, Terri was given a positive review and a raise. As such, she suspected that her employer, who is self-insured, found out about her condition, and fired her to avoid the projected expenses.

While the Internet delivers us instant health information at the click of a button, it can also confuse us. The average reading level in this country is somewhat lower than the reading level required for much of the health information stored on the various and sundry sites out there. While consumer sites, such as WebMD, make a heroic effort to be easily readable, the sites most of us uncover using a search engine are anything but. This can lead to confusion which can impede appropriate health care.

Then there are the web sites that sell "cures" for everything. The FTC, FDA and other law enforcement agencies have become aggressive in trying to stop Internet scams for supplements and other products that purport to cure cancer, HIV/AIDS and countless other life-threatening diseases. Unfortunately, even opiates can be bought online.

Sick people are usually desperate often searching the web to find cures when nothing else seems to work. Many of us are smart enough to take what they find with a grain of salt. People like Louise Kohl Leahy,

I knew about the web from the beginning. I started out with CompuServe .... I suddenly realized how anonymous the Web was. You could say you are a doctor and not be .... Having been in graduate school for so many years I knew I could trust the American Cancer Society for information .... What I read on the web got me to keep it up [her therapy]. I found that I was not alone.

For every logical patient like Louise there are the patients that hang onto every dream of a quick cure. According to the Federal Trade Commission, which has filed complaints against several of these companies, people could cancel their legitimate treatments in favor of unproven herbal cures.

The Internet is a powerful medium. It has gotten people to believe some foolish things such as that an electric current would kill the parasites that cause cancer or Alzheimers. Or that those with HIV or AIDS would use St. John's Wort when, in point of fact, it has been proven that this particular herbal remedy actually interferes with proven HIV/AIDS medications.

Colloidal silver is probably the biggest bamboozle of all. A search in turns up 13 million web sites that talk about this product. The FDA and FTC have identified many of these that have made serious drug claims. Fortunately, health surfers can also use the Internet to ask about these same products. This is what Rick did on the MedHelp International hepatitis forum,

My question is about colloidal silver and can it be harmful. I have friends who say this is the answer to most all our health problems. Supposedly no virus can live in its presence after a few minutes. They make it at home and drink anywhere from a teaspoon to an 8 oz. Glass of this daily! I have heard that you can even inject it. It seems to be quite popular around here. I am afraid it could cause some problems ....

The FDA has leaned hard on these web sites by sending out warning letters. In case common sense doesn't kick in automatically (if so, do I have a bridge to sell you) here's some tell-tale signs that should set off the warning bells: testimonials from people who claim amazing results; claims that the product is a "scientific breakthrough" or "miraculous cure" or is an "ancient remedy" or has a "secret ingredient"; claims that the product can cure just about everything; uses impressive sounding medical terms; and claims that the product is available from one single source and that payment is required in advance. Finally, never buy or rely on anything from a web site that fails to list a company name, address and telephone number (in fact it's a good idea to call them up first).

There are thousands of Internet health-related websites. They make for good reading but often bad science.

@UTHOR BIO

Jessica Keyes is the president of New Art Technologies, Inc., a high-technology and management consultancy and development firm started in New York in 1989.

Keyes has given seminars for such prestigious universities as Carnegie Mellon, Boston University, University of Illinois, James Madison University and San Francisco State University. She is a frequent keynote speaker on the topics of competitive strategy and productivity and quality. She is former advisor for DataPro, McGraw-Hill's computer research arm, as well as a member of the Sprint Business Council. Keyes is also a founding Board of Director member of the New York Software Industry Association. She completed a two-year term on the Mayor of New York City's Small Business Advisory Council. She currently facilitates doctoral and other courses for the University of Phoenix and is a member of the Faculty Council for the College of Information Systems & Technology. She has been the editor for WGL's Handbook of eBusiness and CRCPress' Systems Development Management and Information Management.

Prior to founding New Art, Keyes was Managing Director of R&D for the New York Stock Exchange and has been an officer with Swiss Bank Co. and Banker's Trust, both in New York City. She holds a Masters of Business Administration from New York University, and a Doctorate in management. A noted columnist and correspondent with over 200 articles and 35 books.